THE SONG OF MYSELF

The Bhagavad Gita

Also by David Lindley

Ideas of Order
The Freedom to Be Tragic
Something and Nothing: Selected Poems
Book of Days

THE SONG OF MYSELF

A new verse translation of

The Bhagavad Gita

with an introduction, notes on the text
and a concluding essay

by

David Lindley

I too am untranslatable Walt Whitman, *Song of Myself*

Verborum Editions

First published 2015 by Verborum Editions

www.verborumeditions.com

Set in Janson type

Typeset by Sarah Rock

978-1-907100-04-8

CREATION
from the Rig Veda (10.129)

Then
was not
what was not,
was not
what was.
Space was not,
there was no sky above.
What contained it?
Where?
And in whose keeping
was it?
Was there water
then,
unfathomably deep?

There was no death
then,
no immortality.
Nothing to divide
the day from night.
Then
there was only
that,
without breath,
breathed of itself,
the one,
and nothing beyond.

Then
there was darkness
hidden in darkness,
an indistinguishable
ocean.
Then
the one
contained in nothingness
came to be,
born of heat.

Desire
came to it
then,
the first seed
of thought.
And so the poets
with the wisdom of the heart
found out creation
is dependent on the uncreated.

They drew a line
across the void:
but was the one above
or was the one below?
There were sowers of seed
and fertile powers,
appetite below
and the giver above.

But who knows
and who can say
from where it sprang?
Where did creation come from?
The gods came later,
so who knows
how it came to be?

The one who looks down
on it from the highest heaven,
its keeper,
did He make it?
Surely He knows?
And yet
perhaps He does not know...?

INTRODUCTION
THE VOICES OF THE BHAGAVAD GITA

Do I contradict myself?
Very well then I contradict myself,
(I am large, I contain multitudes.) Walt Whitman, *Song of Myself*

In or around the year 120 CE, at the Fourth Buddhist Council of monks in Kashmir, the Buddha was formally declared divine, and much of the accumulated superstitious practices of the laity that had by then grown up around the person of the Buddha were accepted as the inevitable collateral associated with a divine personage. It marked a permanent divide between a devotion to the unified word of the Buddha preserved and transmitted by the Sangha, the Buddhist monastic and lay order, since the time of the Buddha's death in 486 BCE, and the schismatic development of a religion in which the direct understanding of the teaching, the *dharma*, through one's own efforts, increasingly gave way to a simpler form of devotion to the Buddha as the source of divine good will. The intervening 600 years had seen the rise of Buddhism to become the dominant national religion of India under the patronage of Ashoka, beginning around 250 BCE and spreading from the northern states into all parts of southern India. Buddhism's decline in India, and the resurgence of the brahmanic ritual religion (and its interweaving with non-vedic tantric occultism) date from between the time of the Fourth Buddhist Council and the effective demise of Buddhism in India by 700 CE and its final destruction by the invading Muslims in 712 CE, who gave the word 'Hindu' to the peoples of the Sindhu (Indus) river valley. It is more than likely that the *Gita* belongs broadly to this period. Internal evidence from some Buddhist elements in the text, and frequent references to the rigidity of the caste system, would place the oldest version of it no earlier than the first century BCE. We know from recent genetic evidence that the strict adoption of caste laws began to shape *inherited* caste divisions only around the first century CE, with a marked 'shift to endogamy'[1] coinciding with their encoding in what became known as the law code of Manu. Laws generally encode practice, but the mixing of castes, and caste mobility, were the norm up to this time, so Arjuna's fear of caste corruption (which was solely a concern of the Brahmins) expressed in the opening setting of the *Gita* cannot have dated from much earlier. As an acceptable brahmanic answer to the hegemony of Buddhism, the *Gita* can justify the assimilation of some of the apparently contradictory non-brahmanic elements into the received text, including the much later Vaishnava colouring that, while inimical to the purely ritual-based religion of the Brahmins, none the less offered a response to Buddhist devotional worship that could at least remain within the widening sphere of Brahmin influence and control. The commentary of Shankara, dating from around 800 CE, demarcates the possible outer limit of the *Gita's* final recension as a composite, syncretic work that, though uncanonical in relation to the vedic religion, serves in its ecumenical way to satisfy the Brahmin orthodoxy, and the Brahmin ownership of a wisdom whose origins may lie outside it.

A recurring image in the Upanishads is of the 'imperishable' *one* spinning out threads like the spider, to which the *many* are attached, spinning them out and withdrawing them again. The *Gita*, too, is connected by threads to the many, to the multiple influences of a distant past and to an equally distant future of numerous subsequent interpretations, in a complex web that will always deny the *Gita* a singularity of meaning and a simple integrity.

---

[1] Moorjani, Priya, Kumarasamy Thangaraj, Nick Patterson, Mark Lipson, Po-Ru Loh, Periyasamy Govindaraj, Bonnie Berger, David Reich, and Lalji Singh. "Genetic Evidence for Recent Population Mixture in India." *The American Journal of Human Genetics* 93, no. 3 (2013): 422-38.

The *Gita* exists because the Vedas exist. The oldest of the four Vedas, the *Rig Veda*, may have been composed before the Aryas migrated to northern India, bringing with them their gods of the natural world, the hymns and rites of sacrifice, celebration and propitiation. The gods are born from the sacrifice, and the Vedas are *'shruti'*, the 'heard' formulation of the word and its metre that binds the gods to the sacrifice from the beginning of time. Along with their gods, the Aryas brought with them the class divisions that were to become the castes of Indian society, led by the princely tribal warriors of the *kshatriya* caste, with their horses and their chariots, and accompanied by the Brahmins, the hearers of the word and its singers and reciters, in which, and therefore in whom, all divine power rested.

The Vedas were not the written word but the uttered word, the remembered word. The Brahmin (*'brahman'*) was he who knew the word and exclusively controlled the power of the word, the 'holy word' (also *'brahman'*). The word of the Brahmin was a source of power for kings, princes and warriors, and the patronage of royalty was in turn a source of the Brahmin's own power: 'verily by means of the holy power he quickens the kingly power, and by the kingly power the holy power; therefore a Brahman who has a princely person is superior to another Brahman; therefore a prince who has a Brahman is superior to another prince.'[1] *'Brahman'* was 'the highest realm of speech'[2] the power of which was vested in the enchantment of the metre itself.[3] The word is the sound of the indivisible truth of things, whose essence is contained in the chanted syllable 'OM', the 'quintessence of all essences'.[4]

The vedic religion was never to lose sight of the underlying unity of phenomena. The gods themselves

---

[1] *Yajur Veda* 5.1.10
[2] *Yajur Veda* 7.4.18
[3] *Yajur Veda* 2.6.9
[4] *Chandogya Upanishad* 1.1.2 (Olivelle)

were born from the one original self-sacrifice of the world's creator, Prajapati, and man and all living creatures are distributions of the original man, Purusha. That essential unity is not only a characteristic of the primitive religion, but persists in the character of later Hinduism as what Zaehner[1] called 'pantheistic monism' and Chaudhuri, following him, chose to refer to as 'polymorphous monotheism'. One early manifestation of that unity is the idea of 'breath'. It permeates the vedic verses, both as the support of the universe and the essence of life, at once 'the lord of all that breathes and does not breathe'.[2] Breath is not only 'lord of all' but 'no other than my self'. The word *atman*, the self, which is to feature so prominently in the Upanishads and the *Gita*, is etymologically connected to the Greek *atmos* and retains the idea of 'wind' or 'breath'. In the sound world of the vedic mind, words do not *stand for* things but are the equivalents of things, just as, in the primitive mind, gods are not representations of things, of wind or fire or water or thunder, but the things themselves in the poetic forms of subjective experience. No one thing is divorced from another, or from its origins, but has an indissoluble grammar. In this same hymn to breath (*prana*) in the *Atharva Veda*, we find an illustration of the sustaining power of the *one* in the imagery of the swan rising from the water. The swan, as it breaks free of the surface of the lake, always trails one foot at the point at which it takes flight. If it were to withdraw that foot, says the verse, 'never would there be today, tomorrow, nor the night, nor day, and never would the dawn come'. In a world where the word is the equivalent of the thing itself, where the flight of the swan is dependent upon the same operational power that sustains both the universe and the self, the grammar of speech and the coherence of experience are one continuum.

By the time of the Aryan settlement, the Indus Valley

[1] Zaehner, R. C. *Hindu Scriptures*. Everyman's Library, 1992.
[2] *Atharva Veda* 11.4

civilisation which had preceded it was in decline and had already moved steadily eastwards and south, mixing with the aboriginal population, taking with it the symbols of its own religious heritage from Mesopotamia, among them the horned god seated in a yoga posture, the prototype of the god Shiva, 'Lord of Yoga'. Theirs was an agrarian, village-based culture but with known urban administrative centres at Harappa and Mohenjo-daro, where the archaeological record shows a civilisation skilled in the management of the water supply, and in the construction of tanks, indications, perhaps, of the early origins of ritual bathing that prevails throughout the subcontinent. The Aryas, by contrast, lighter skinned and 'noble' ('*aryan*'), with their horses, cattle and goats by which they measured their wealth, constituted a 'barbarian' invasion. Did these outward-looking ritual worshippers of their gods, interbreeding over the next several centuries with the indigenous population, at some point, perhaps around 600 BCE, encounter what Joseph Campbell called 'an alien constellation' of quieter, more introspective lines of thinking about man's place in the universe, not a line initiated by the Brahmins but one already the province of the princes of an earlier ruling class?

The Upanishads are filled with stories of challenging encounters between Brahmins of the vedic culture and other, alien voices debating the nature of true knowledge, in which the gods themselves wonder at the power of this new being, *brahman*. What is *brahman*? Not what you think it is, but something only 'seen by one who sees it not':

> *That which one breathes without breath,*
> *that by which breath is breathed,*
> *that alone is brahman,*
> *not what they worship here as that.*[1]

---

[1] *Kena Upanishad* 1.8, based on Hume

The Upanishads, literally meaning the 'hidden connections' of doctrine, present a synthesis of the new knowledge and the ritual foundation of the vedic sacrifice. There is a 'hidden connection' to *brahman* and 'austerities, restraint and the rites are its foundation, the [four] Vedas its four limbs'.[1] The *Gita* is also an Upanishad, in which we find a claim to the royal lineage of a 'secret' doctrine. None the less, the doctrine's elaboration in the Upanishad literature into the world-view of the unity of *brahman* and *atman*, the self, and, in the late Upanishads and the Vaishnavite elements of the *Gita*, the unity of *brahman-atman* with God, was the product of brahmanic thought, speculation and discourse. All wisdom, all knowledge, all learning is the exclusive domain of the Brahmin.

Over a short period of time, perhaps no more than 200 years, the Brahmin witnessed the persistence of the 'new' *brahman*, the development of the *samkhya* school of philosophy along with its various associated schools of yoga, the emergence of Buddhism and the parallel ascetic practices of the Jains. Not one of these constellations of thought and practice arose directly out of the vedic ritual religion, and none of them had a theistic foundation. Matter and spirit came first, and this duality of the essence of things preceded the gods who were derived from it. If the gods are essential to the running of the world, they are complicit in the round of existence, and their worship simply binds man to that eternally revolving wheel. The gods are irrelevant to man's salvation, to his final escape, to *moksha* or *nirvana*. The gods may connect you to the worlds of heaven and hell, to life and death, to sleep and dream, to rewards and punishments, but they cannot give you freedom.

Brahmanism responded to this upsurge of non-vedic, often contra-vedic thinking, not by resisting it but by

---

[1] *Kena Upanishad* 4.8

accommodating it without surrendering the vedic foundation of the new synthesis. The Veda might be transcended by the 'wise Brahmin' who understood, interpreted and taught the new learning, but it remained the source of brahmanic authority. *Brahman, atman, samkhya*, yoga, and elements of Buddhism were adopted into what became known as the later Veda, or the Vedanta, united by the authority of the Brahmin's voice, which has never learned the virtue of the silence that sits at the heart of Buddhism: 'Better the speaking than the silent Brahmin,' says the *Rig Veda*. By the time we arrive at Shankara, the first commentator of the *Gita*, the subject of the speaking Brahmin is God. Both Buddhism and Jainism had become, at least in the popular mind and in devotional practice, theistic religions. Christianity, and then Islam, had established the unbreachable belief in the one God and Supreme Being and creator, and Hinduism had assumed to itself in the many faces of the gods the underlying unity of the One. In the late *Shvetashvatara Upanishad* we find all these elements woven together with joyously confused enthusiasm: the highest God among gods who is the Lord, the master of the universe, the first cause and controller, the Benign One, the ruler of both *brahman* and *atman*, with whom we become united through the practice of *samkhya-yoga*, but also through worship, devotion and adoration. Here we have all the threads that connect the *Gita* itself backward in time to the original received word of the Veda, given at the beginning of creation, forward via *samkhya-yoga* doctrine to its great Vaishnavite advocate, Shankara, and on until it reaches the sympathetic ear of its first European translators who add their voices, echoing their own theistic and spiritual inheritance, to this polyphonic text.

The voices of the *Gita* never quite harmonise. It is as well to recognise this at the outset to avoid mistaking for contradictions several different ideas that manage to live side by side in the devotional text of the *Gita*, just as divergent religious beliefs live side by side in an Indian village, united by a common necessity to believe and the single idea of the saving power of devotion. There are three different strands running through the *Gita*, three voices that do most of the speaking. The first, and the dominant of these is that of the teacher.

The *Gita* opens, following the prelude describing the setting on the battlefield in the *Mahabharata* epic, as a question and answer dialogue between the wise, enlightened teacher, exponent of *samkhya* knowledge and proponent of *samkhya-yoga*, specifically *karma-yoga* theory and practice, and his novitiate. The role of the pupil, seeking an answer to the moral problem of action, and ultimately seeking also to acquire an understanding of the teaching and to adopt the disciplined way of yoga, is given to Arjuna, a *kshatriya* warrior in the larger epic narrative. The role of teacher is given to Krishna, a *kshatriya* prince and sometime *avatara* of Vishnu in his incremental role as the focus of the later Vishnu cult. In this intellectual strand of the *Gita*, Arjuna is merely the counterpoint to the teacher, there only in order to frame the questions the teacher needs to answer to develop the doctrine. He plays only a nominal role as the seeker of wisdom. The teacher has a more developed personality, wise, knowledgeable, analytical, intuitive, and often scathing, capable of great eloquence on behalf of *brahman* and the *atman* of which and for whom he speaks.

We can follow the track of the teaching and its development through the text, a text interrupted by frequent brahmanic exegesis, which contributes the second noticeable voice to the *Gita*, and disrupted by the easily identifiable insertions of the Vaishnava *bhakti* sectarians, who contribute the third voice we hear. It begins, at 2.11, by establishing the eternality, and the wonder, of the self embodied within a material and perishable form. Once you understand the self, it says, you will see that it is neither slain (in the context of the conflict about to take place) nor the slayer, since the self (as will become clearer) is not the agent of action. One should act and perform one's duty as a material being. The self is indifferent to success or failure. This teaching is announced as a tenet of the *samkhya* doctrine. It now adds some further points: you must take up the arduous path of yoga practice to free the self from the delusion of being tied to its actions, and it vocally opposes this way to the numerous ways of others who are tied to *ritual* actions and pleased with their flowery interpretation of the Vedas. It then explains and extols the necessity of detaching the self from action, in particular from the performance of the rites, and from both the motives and the hoped for fruits of action. How might that level of detachment be achieved? asks the pupil. By yoga discipline, explains the master, bringing us to the conclusion of Book 2.

In the opening verses of Book 3 the master answers another question, a critical one to understanding the whole teaching. If right knowledge and right understanding are opposed to action, why should I act? The answer is that there are two ways of yoga in the *samkhya*, one focused purely on acquiring knowledge, in pursuit of which a man divorces himself from the world (the reflective way of the forest hermit), and the other permitting action in the world based on a true understanding of the nature of action and the self. But both are knowledge-based in the first place. This whole teaching of *karma-yoga*, in a nutshell, concludes at 3:9:

> *This world is such*
> *that action cannot be avoided.*
> *The only action that is free*
> *is worship.*
> *Do this freely.*

The teaching related to non-attachment resumes at 3:17,

and at 3:36 identifies 'desire' as the root cause of all our troubles. It is the enemy, but something stands above it, the self, its potential conqueror.

With Book 4 the teaching takes another direction. The doctrine, we learn, is a 'secret doctrine' with a royal heritage, an older way of thinking that periodically goes into decline and has to be resurrected. This teaches *'brahman'* as the non-acting but sustaining ground of the world. What is meant by action and non-action, and the nature of agency, is difficult to understand and, it declares, widely misunderstood. Through the practice of non-attachment the self learns that it, too, does not act. Its final act is to sacrifice the illusion of the acting self.

Book 5 picks up where the rather fragmentary Book 4 leaves off, returning to the 'two ways' of yoga, the purely reflective way and the way that permits action, and explaining further how to renounce attachment to actions, desires, motivations and ends. That theme continues through to 6:28 where the central teaching relating to the detachment of the self from action reaches a natural conclusion.

At this point the subject changes to the oneness of the self and *brahman*, realised through self-mastery and devotion to the way of knowledge and yoga discipline so far expounded. The self and its actions are to be surrendered to *brahman*, for the non-acting self is the same as the non-acting ground of the world. These ideas reach a high point in Book 7 where the master, now transfigured as *brahman-atman*, declares his higher universal nature that has been hidden by his 'lower' nature, his material composition and the actions of a man's will and character that are part of that nature. Book 8 delves into these questions further, clearly distinguishing the 'dark' path followed by material natures attached to their desires and to the 'old' dogmas of the vedic ritual, a path which leads inexorably to rebirth and the common round of repeated existence, and the 'light' path to enlightenment and freedom through single-minded devotion to the true teaching. From Book 8 through to the end of Book 12, that devotional aspect begins to predominate, reaching its apotheosis in the purely Vaishnavite interpolations of Books 10 and 11.

Book 13 is the first in a series of rather more technical treatments of the *samkhya* philosophy, and provides a more analytical approach to understanding action and non-action and the self as the non-acting conscious 'witness' of the world and its unfolding activity. We are back to the core teaching, at a deeper level. This is probably the most profound section of the *Gita*, clarifying in a very definitive way the difference between man's material nature and his embodied self, between the material world sustained by a single principle, *brahman*, and knowledge of the world sustained by a single 'knower', the self. It contains in brief the entire journey from ignorance to understanding, from attachment to liberation, from the delusion of disunity to the realisation of the highest form of integrity.

Book 14 presents a further exegesis of the *samkhya* theory of the *gunas*, the 'qualities', those inherent temperaments of character in the material self that are the real source of men's actions. The self is able to transcend them, but only by subduing their influence through renunciation of the preferences they inspire in the individual personality. The delineation of the character of the transcendent man begun towards the end of Book 14 is continued in Book 16 (Book 15 being an odd miscellany of assertions already made elsewhere) which goes on to present a powerful indictment of the 'demonic' man who opposes the self in his own heart and who is satisfied to embrace the impulses of his material nature as all that there is of value in this world. Book 17 is entirely devoted to a thesis on the three *gunas* in their various manifestations, linked back to the explanations begun in Book 14, with a particular emphasis on how they determine individual approaches to worship and austerities.

The final chapter of the *Gita* does succeed in bringing together all the components of the teaching, explaining again quite clearly the nature of action and non-action, the role of the *gunas* in action, and the supremacy of the self that is free from action once the follower of this teaching has renounced the motivations and the fruits of actions as his own to become at peace within himself and at one with both *brahman* and with the self that is the same in every being. The teaching concludes at 18:54.

Although the teaching declares itself antithetical to the older vedic ritual religion, the Brahmin will always have the last word: not to oppose the new learning or justify his own position, but to elaborate his position as the most learned among the learned. The core teaching of the *Gita* presents a 'higher' knowledge and a 'supreme' goal, neither of which can be denied. But the Veda is the base, the immutable foundation of that higher wisdom, a means to an end; and if the Vedas can be surpassed, dispensed with, as so much overflowing water in a deep well of wisdom, then the learned Brahmin will extend his learning to embrace that higher teaching. His voice is always present to expand, amplify or elaborate virtually every mention of the rites and sacrifices in the *Gita*, adding and correcting detail and ensuring that even where we are asked to disregard the Vedas they retain their eternal authority at the heart of all that has been taught since. While that voice for the most part weaves in and out of the verse sequences, in some places it is possible to discern where specific brahmanic commentary has been inserted. One example occurs at 3:10. Verse 3:9 ends by asserting that the only action the self is permitted to perform is the act of sacrifice (translated here as 'worship'). That immediately sets off a sequence of verses devoted to the eternal nature of the sacrifice, upon which even *brahman* is dependent, before the interrupted discourse on action resumes at 3:17.

We hear, too, if not the voice of the Brahmin (who

owns all vedic knowledge) then the voice of the *pandit*, frequently referred to throughout the *Gita*, the learned doctor of esoteric knowledge. He it is, perhaps, who descants on the way of the moon and the solar pathway to rebirth, through the dark way of smoke or the light way of fire, a doctrinal exposition unrelated to the Vedas, belonging rather to an alternative esoteric lore that makes its appearance in the *Chandogya Upanishad*, which occupies the last six verses of Book 8.

The third voice we hear is the voice of God, or rather the fervent voices of the later theistic interpreters of the intuitive understanding of the unity of *brahman* and *atman*. The core *samkhya-yoga* teaching in the *Gita* is concerned with liberating the non-acting self from the 'not-self' that believes it is the agent and conscience of its actions by firstly, through both intellectual understanding and yogic discipline and practice, detaching the self from the sources of its motivations to act by recognising and overcoming the *gunas* of an entirely material self. The product of that disciplined understanding is an equanimity of mind, similar to the *apatheia* of the Greek Stoics and the *ataraxia* of the Sceptics, when one has finally realised that there can be nothing in the outer phenomena of the world to trouble us, and that our disquiet arises solely from the emotional shaping of ourselves and our self-interests to the objects of our desires on the one hand, or our aversions on the other. That teaching is then further developed and melded into a doctrine of self-realisation that takes the self to its ultimate goal of recognising that the self and *brahman* have the same eternal non-acting qualities, that they are one, and we are thereby released not only from action but from the cause of our continual enslavement to the round of birth and death. Because we are free, in life, of that mortal coil we are, in reality, immortal. There are just two dimensions to that understanding: *brahman*, as the beginning, middle and end of all phenomena, and *atman*, the enduring cognitive self. One is the *that* of the objective world, the other the *this* of subjective experience. They are both unborn, without qualities, without attachments, unending and, as such, realisable as one. Since they are in reality *one*, it makes the casting of the *Gita* as a theistic work not only possible but easy. Once that third dimension of the *one* God has been introduced, it is only a matter of formal augmentation and argumentation to render the one, not as the identification of the two as one, but as a third all-subsuming one that is the home, the womb, the giver, the director and controller of the other two. This is what we encounter explicitly in the *Shvetashvatara Upanishad*, the over-excited theistic cousin of the *Gita*, and again in the commentary on the *Gita* by Shankara. Shankara simply *produces* God, *ex machina*, who is the creator, Vishnu, incarnate as Krishna, the Lord, the First Cause, embodied but really 'unborn and indestructible... the Lord of Creatures, Eternal, Pure, Intelligent and Free',[1] returned to earth to preserve the vedic religion upon which the distinction of the Brahmin and the hierarchy of caste are dependent. 'Me', in the Gita, for Shankara means 'Vishnu, the Supreme Lord' [7:5] and 'the very *brahman*, the very self' in the heart of all [9:14]. God (Vishnu) is at once the Supreme Self, unconditioned *brahman* and the Lord of the Universe [Book 12]. *Brahman* and the self are both contained in God [14:27], one becomes *brahman* by the 'Grace and Mercy of the Lord' [14:26] and 'seeing that All is Vasudeva [God], he becomes Vasudeva'. [14:19]

The theistic, and specifically Vaishnavite interpolations are very apparent. The theistic ground is otherwise largely a matter of interpretation of a teaching cast in the form of a first person declamation. The interpolated

---

[1] Sastri, A. Mahadeva. *The Bhagavad-Gita with the Commentary of Sri Sankaracharya.* 2nd ed. Mysore, 1901, p.4. The references in brackets that follow are to the chapter commentary of Shankara in the same work.

passages are substantially the adulatory section running from 10:12 through to 11:54 which stands out distinctly from the surrounding text. There are also additional verses tacked not very convincingly onto the end of Book 18, which had effectively concluded at 18:54. The most obvious evidence of the appropriation of the *Gita* by the Vishnu cult lies in the title itself, 'The Song Sung by the Lord', and in the recurrence of the phrasing 'the Blessed Lord spoke' to introduce those parts of the discourse voiced by Krishna. Nowhere outside the Vaishnavite portions of the *Gita* does Krishna claim to be God. But he does speak authoritatively in the first person, which permits the theistic reading, and we need briefly to account for that.

Brahman is (objectively) unconditioned, without qualities, unknowable. The self, too, in reality, is unconditioned and without qualities, and in this respect is one with *brahman*, but, as subject-in-itself, is the only knower of *brahman*. Therefore it is the self that speaks, and it is only the self that may speak, and the self naturally speaks in the first person, the first person being both *atman* and *brahman* who, between them, bestride the entire universe in its conscious and unconscious manifestation. There is no room for, and no necessity for a third, so to speak, first person, higher than either and the creator and controller of both, the arbitrary giver and taker away of grace and favour. No one in reality can speak for this third first person except the original first person who conceived Him, who is the only authority for the subjective knowledge of Him and on whom even God depends for His thoughts. The self identified with the universe is 'all', and speaks for all unconditionally. We cannot hear the words of God, we can only hear our own words cast back upon us in the measure of their truthfulness.

Translation is an original act of creation. When we read, whether we realise it or not, we recreate a part of the external and objective world of words as an internal and subjective, personal and original world of meaning. When we reread a book it does not have the same meaning. Translation is the art of rereading, and if the words settle on the page with the apparent finality of objectivity, this is merely the illusion of the reader.

The *Gita* presents particular difficulties for both the reader and the translator. Its meaning is unclear because no single, easily expressible meaning is intended. Like the epic poems of Homer it has no known author to give it a singular authoritative voice. The Sanskrit language itself allows multiple meanings to attach themselves to single words or word combinations. And words are only the surface sediment of a deep evolutionary history of their meaning. They lie scattered on the surface of the text like so many cultural artefacts whose original usage is now obscure. There can be no definitive translation of the *Gita*. One can only translate the *Gita* as a reading of the text, with the personal interpretation of meaning that defines the act of reading.

My relationship with the text is a personal one. In undertaking a translation I have hoped to make my own ideas clear by attempting to make clear the main ideas and tenets found in the *Gita*, and where those ideas are not clear, or are not ideas at all but intuitive assertions, or poetic excursions, or gnomic utterances, or interpolated commentary, I have let them stand as such. Not all crooked things need to be made straight, and a singular truth is less interesting than our numberless attempts at it. I have, in the process, made a number of 'hidden connections' of my own between those attempts in the accompanying notes to the text by situating the book in hand among other books whose voices, too, speak of 'the two old, simple problems ever intertwined', life and death.[1] Walt Whitman's was one of those voices that

---

[1] Walt Whitman, *Life and Death* in *Leaves of Grass*, 1892.

spoke loudly and most to the point, and I have taken lines from his *Song of Myself* as appropriate epigraphs for each of the chapters of the *Gita*, to argue for the universality of the first person freed from its narrowness of interest, waiting to be found in more than one place:

> *Missing me one place search another,*
> *I stop somewhere waiting for you.*

I have not tried to reproduce in English the unique sound world of the metres of the Sanskrit verses (which are quantitative, as in Greek and Latin verse) intended to be sung, not spoken or read. Instead, the metre is the natural iambic rhythm of English prosody, more correctly a disrupted iambic, or its mirror the trochaic, with occasional rhythmic variations where it seemed appropriate. The Sanskrit verses have four lines. They are generally very compact, with the metre and the sound values tending to take precedence over the meaning: the frequent inclusion of epithets for either Arjuna or Krishna, the use of 'filler' words such as the Sanskrit equivalents of 'even' or 'also' to maintain the metre, the inclusion of a word or its positioning for euphony, the choice of word for its length or sound value and the deliberate indulgence in verbal antithesis, often leave little room for the unequivocal development of the full import of the meaning. That concision can often be effectively reproduced in English, but more frequently it becomes necessary to expand the line to make good sense. While retaining the verse numbering, I have not kept to the four line form of the verses and have run some verses together where either the lines in the original spill over into the next verse or it is helpful to connect a train of thought into one sequence. Many of those sequences, and a number of individual verses, are disconnected from either the previous or the following verses. I have indicated the most easily isolated of these with separating asterisks. The *Gita* meanders, repeats itself, reformulates verses, steps aside to explore a liturgical byway; it is not a narrative with a beginning, middle and end, and it may be easier to piece together a coherent whole if the reader can more easily recognise breaks in continuity.

I have tried to make the verses readable and melodic without sacrificing the literal value of each word in the original. Where I have glossed the line I have made that clear in the notes. The line arrangement is very variable. I break a line where it seems called for, or to denote a change in the rhythm, or to draw the reader's attention to a particular point or individual word. In writing the opening verses, set in the epic context of the *Mahabharata*, I fell in with echoes of the literary heritage of Greek, German, Icelandic epic and saga and, inevitably, the sonorities of the King James Bible. For the hymn to Vishnu that fills out Books 10 and 11 I have employed a more archaic and stilted language in keeping with older, nineteenth and early twentieth century reverential literature in English, including some earlier translations of the *Gita*. Needless to say, those variations in style are not reflections of the original, though more than one formal metrical arrangement is used in the Sanskrit verses. To confess the other few liberties I have taken: I have given the work a variant title that I think is in keeping with the central doctrine of the *Gita* to replace the familiar Vaishnava one; provided chapter headings from a line of verse in each chapter; and, to improve the flow, I have excised, with a few exceptions, the introductory lines 'Arjuna spoke' and 'The Blessed Lord spoke', indicating by additional line spacing the change of speaker.

The use of diacritics in the transliteration of Sanskrit seemed to me over-pedantic when the few names and terms present in the translation offer very little difficulty in pronunciation. I have transcribed the sibilants 'ś' and 'ṣ' as 'sh': Kṛṣna is always Krishna; *sudra* becomes *shudra* and *vaisya* becomes *vaishya*. I have adopted the usual stem forms of *brahman* and *atman*, but employed the nominative *karma* rather than *karman* to reflect common usage. I have translated these and other terms where possible and where it makes sense to do so, but where the text deals extensively with their definition or description (as it does in particular for the three *gunas*) I have left them untranslated and in italic.

The word '*brahman*' stands for the all-pervasive sustaining principle of the universe; but it is also the correct formulation for both the priestly *brahman* caste as a whole and for the individual practising *brahman*. It is also used to mean the 'holy power' of the word of the Vedas. To avert some of the confusion that arises from these multiple occurrences I have reverted to the older, if no longer correct, Anglicised 'Brahmin' for the caste and for the 'priesthood', but continued to use 'brahmanic' as the adjectival form.

THE SONG OF MYSELF

The Bhagavad Gita

1

PROLOGUE: IN SORROW AND DESPAIR

Battles, the horrors of fratricidal wars, the fever of doubtful news,
the fitful events Walt Whitman, *Song of Myself*

1:1 And blind King Dhritarashtra said:
Tell me what befell upon the Kuru field,
the field of duty,
where my sons and Pandu's sons,
eager for battle, stood to fight.

1:2 Then the seer Sanjaya said:
O King, your son Prince Duryodhana,
seeing the sons of Pandu thus arrayed for war,
turned to his master, Drona, skilled in arms,
and said to him:
1:3 O Master, look upon the sons of Pandu
and their armies ranged in battle order
by the son of Drupada whose martial skills
he got from you!
1:4 Here stand heroes and great archers,
equals of the mighty Bhima, equal unto Arjuna:
Yuyudhana the unconquerable, King Virata,
Drupada himself, commander of the great war car.
1:5 Dhrishtaketu, Chekitana, the valiant King of Kashi,
Purujit of Kuntibhoja, Shaibya, king and best of men,
1:6 Yudhamanju, Uttamaujas, heroes both,
Subhadra's son, the sons of Draupadi,
every one a mighty war car warrior.

1:7 Now let me name our forces,

O best among the twice born,
that you may know them and who leads them.

1:8   You, your noble self, and Bhishma,
Karna and the undefeated Kripa,
Ashvatthama and Vikarna and Somadatta's son

1:9   and many other heroes armed with many arms
and gifted in the arts of war, ready to die for me.

1:10   We are the lesser force
but have wise Bhishma to protect us,
and though they are the greater force
Bhima is less skilled than Bhishma.

1:11   And so let each in his appointed place
in turn guard Bhishma and protect him.

1:12   And then did Bhishma, valorous elder of the Kuru clan,
give heart to Duryodhana with a lion's roar
and blew a blast upon his conch-shell.

1:13   And all at once tumultuous
became the sound of conches,
cow-horns, clashing cymbals
and the beating drums of war.

1:14   Then standing on their mighty chariot
harnessed to white horses
Krishna and the son of Pandu
blew their godlike conches.

1:15   Krishna blew the conch-horn Panchajanya,
Arjuna sounded Devadatta,
and wolflike Bhima, terrible in deeds,
took up the great shell Paundra.

1:16   Prince Yudishthira blew Anantavijaya,
Nakula and Sahadeva blew Sughosha
and the conch-shell Manipushpaka.

1:17   And the valiant archer, King of Kashi,
and Shikhandi, great chariot warrior,

Dhrishtadyumna and Virata
and unconquered Satyaki,

1:18   Drupada and the sons of Draupadi,
and Subhadra's strong-armed son,
all loudly blew their conch-shells,

1:19   rending earth from sky and tearing
at the hearts of Dhritarashtra's men.

1:20   Now, as the clash of arms began,
Arjuna lifted up his bow.
But seeing Dhritarashtra's men
arrayed for battle

1:21   spoke these words to Krishna:
Draw up and halt my chariot
between both armies,

1:22   that I might see all these
who are assembled here,
my enemies in war,

1:23   and know what sort of men
are eager for the joys of battle
for the sake of Dhritarashtra's evil-minded son.

1:24   And Krishna, having heard these words,
drew up that best of chariots between the armies,

1:25   and facing Bhishma, Drona and,
it seemed, the kings of all the world,
he said: O son of Pritha, see before you
all the Kuru clan.

1:26   And Arjuna beheld among them
fathers, elders, teachers,
sons and brothers, uncles,

1:27   grandsons, friends and followers.

1:28   And seeing them, he grieved,
and full of sorrow spoke these words:
O, Krishna, seeing all my kinsmen

here before me, readied for battle,

1:29 my legs fail me and I pale,
my body trembles and my hair
stands up in dread,

1:30 my bow Gandiva slips from my hand,
and my skin burns. I cannot stand,
my mind's distracted

1:31 by such terrible forebodings,
for nothing good can come
of slaying my own kinsmen
in the heat of battle.

1:32 I now have no desire for victory,
for kingdoms or for pleasures.
What use are they

1:33 when those with whom we share our joys
are gathered here to give up life itself:

1:34 teachers, fathers, sons
and brothers, elders, husbands,
men who are my family and kinsmen?

1:35 I will not kill them, demon slayer,
not for heaven or earth, not
even if I die myself.

1:36 By slaying Dhritarashtra's sons,
what good will follow, Krishna,
troubler of evil men?
In slaughtering the wicked
we bring evil on ourselves.

1:37 And so we should not kill them,
for how could we be happy then?

1:38 Though they, on their side,
blinded by their greed,
may see no evil in destroying
family and betraying friends,

1:39 we who are wiser
should turn aside from wickedness,

for nothing is more evil
than this crime against our own.

1:40   Destroy the family, destroy the clan,
and we destroy the sacred laws
of kinship. Destroy the laws,
and lawlessness must follow.

1:41   Without the laws that bind us
women are corrupted.
From their defilement
comes the mixing of the castes.

1:42   Degradation of the caste
leads straight to hell
for family and ancestors alike,
for the holy rites and offerings will cease.

1:43   Such evil and corruption will destroy
eternal laws of caste and family,

1:44   and when these are destroyed,
time and time again I've heard
that hell is certain.

1:45   How great a sin this is,
to take up arms against ourselves
for greed, ambition and the wealth of kings.

1:46   It would be better if
the sons of Dhritarashtra
killed me, unresisting,
weaponless upon this field.

1:47   Thus Arjuna spoke,
and in the midst of battle,
letting fall his arrows and his bow,
sat down in sorrow and despair.

NOTES ON THE TEXT AND TRANSLATION

The war setting described in the opening verses is a war of succession between a family divided against itself in pursuit of power and the legitimacy of the opposing claims to it. The justness of the case on either side is tenuous, both claims serving as the justification for what is in reality a desire for power, wealth and pleasure.

The protagonists in the battle about to unfold are all members of the Kuru royal clan. As the narrative opens the *de facto* king is the blind Dhritarashtra, the elder brother of the dead ruler Pandu with whom he shared power. As the elder brother, Dhritarashtra always had a legitimate claim to rule, but his blindness from birth prohibited him that recognition. On the death of Pandu, Pandu's eldest son Yudisthira should have succeeded him, but of course there is a justification for declaring Dhritarashtra's eldest son Duryodhana the legitimate ruler. Dhritarashtra continued as regent because at the time of Pandu's death Yudisthira was still a boy. As time went on, Dhritarashtra succumbed to the plotting of Duryodhana to assert his right to power, creating the conditions for conflict.

It is in fact the burning ambition of Duryodhana that has ignited the war. Although in point of law and principle his claim may be the most just, he is portrayed here as the least deserving because of his scheming and 'evil minded' personality, in contrast to the more noble characters of Yudisthira and his brother Arjuna. In the narrative Dhritarashtra's party is referred to as the Kauravas, the Kurus or the 'sons of Kuru'. The other side is described as the Pandavas, Pandus or 'sons of Pandu'. Krishna, as this part of the story opens, is the charioteer and intimate of the warrior Arjuna.

Since that epic beginning is largely a device to induct everything that follows into the already extant epic *Mahabharata*, its function as a bridge to the opening dialogue on the subject of action and the self as the agent of action makes it something of an independent unit. It serves to set up the moral 'problem' out of which the subsequent dialogue will grow, and though the unlikelihood of such a philosophical exchange in the midst of war has often been remarked upon, the realism of the setting is less important to the teaching that follows than the reality of the moral conflict that arises from it.

This first book of the *Gita* employs a number of epithets to stand in place of or to supplement many of the names of the protagonists, similar to the Homeric epithets that may already be familiar to the Western reader, such as 'grey-eyed Athena' or 'son of Atreus, tamer of horses' to stand for Agamemnon. In some verses of the *Gita* both the name and the epithet appear in association, as in the first Homeric example, and sometimes the epithet stands alone in place of the person, as in the second example. These are useful devices in the original, both for poetic effect and for cadence, but less useful in translation. A reciter of the *Gita* would, of course, have had a perfect familiarity with all of the characters, their many possible names or epithets (Krishna has, by tradition, at least 108), their history and their destiny, as would the audience since, in a non-literary and hieratic culture, it was meant to be heard only by those qualified to hear it. Translation is a democratising process. There are places in the narrative where we encounter more epithets than we would care to wrestle with; yet there are some verses, including the first two, where an additional descriptive or identifying word or phrase will help the understanding. We might reasonably expect that a recital of the *Gita* for an alien audience might occasionally have incorporated an additional descriptor, and I have occasionally done that.

1:1

blind King. The word 'blind' does not appear in the original text. I have added it here partly to explain the presence of the 'seer' Sanjaya in the next verse as the ostensible narrator of the action and, subsequently, the reciter of the dialogue between Krishna and Arjuna.

the Kuru field, the field of duty. The Kuru field or field of the Kurus (*'kurukshetre'*) is how the site of the battle is named. The opening word of the *Gita* is *'dharmakshetre'*, 'field of duty', and the use of *'dharma'* here has led to some differences of opinion among translators and commentators. Mascaró is insistent that *dharma* should be translated here as 'truth' in the sense of revealed truth or, as he says, 'the Truth of the universe'. But in Sanskrit *dharma* is used in a different sense in different contexts. In the *Gita* it invariably denotes the 'duty' to which each individual being is destined in the continuous round of birth of death. It has been variously translated in this verse as the field of 'law', 'justice', 'right' or 'righteousness'. There is certainly a moral right to be defended, and a warrior's duty to be observed, that justifies this usage, but there is no rationale for believing that the *Gita* opens with a declaration that there is a spiritual truth at stake. The most straightforward translation of *dharmakshetre* is 'sacred field', adopted by Prabhavananda and Isherwood, as the place upon which these historical events and this 'sacred dialogue' (18:70) were deemed to have unfolded.

1:2

seer. I have added this epithet to show the role of Sanjaya here as the 'seer' of the blind king Dhritarashtra, who by the agency of his magical powers sees the action that has taken place, and recites the dialogue between Arjuna and Krishna, though not actually present on either occasion.

Drona is master in the arts of war and has been the teacher
and instructor of Arjuna and of other clan warriors. He is not
mentioned by name in the Sanskrit text, but only as 'teacher'
or, perhaps more correctly, 'master'.

1:3
Drupada is a king in the *Mahabharata* story, once a friend but
now the 'mortal enemy' of Drona. His son is Dhrishtadyumna.
Drona has taught the skills of armed combat to sons who are
now combatants on opposing sides.

1:4
Bhima is the second of the five Pandava brothers (Arjuna is
the third), noted in the *Mahabharata* for his strength and,
later in the epic, as the nemesis of the Kauravas. *Yuyudhana*
(also called Satyaki) is a commander in the Pandava army
and known by his fearful epithet 'unconquerable'. *Virata* is
an ally of the Pandavas.

1:5
All epics, by their very nature, treat of epic events in the
lives of gods and heroes who live on a scale beyond the
achievement of ordinary folk. They inhabit echoing halls
and jewelled palaces, they govern vast kingdoms and rule
multitudes of men. The recital of the names of heroes, kings
and princes, and the conjuring up of the magical names of
their shields and weapons serve to ennoble the mean spirits
of ordinary mortals and turn defeat and the anonymity of
death into remembered tragedy. Epic poetry, as Peter Levi
has said of Homer, 'belongs to the defeated and the dead'.[1]
That naming of heroes, kings, clan members, their allies
and their legendary instruments of war continues in this and
subsequent verses of the epic opening chapter.

[1] *Levi, Peter.* Virgil: His Life and times. *New York: St. Martin's Press, 1999.*

Dhrishtaketu is a tribal king and ally of the Pandavas; *Chekitana* is his son. *Kashi* is the present day Varanasi (Benares).

Purujit of Kuntibhoja. There is some uncertainty as to whether Purujit and Kuntibhoja are one or two persons. Kuntibhoja is the adoptive father of Kunti (known as Pritha, the mother of the three elder Pandava brothers) and presumably an old man at this time. It seems likely that Purujit, brother of Kunti and maternal uncle of the Pandavas, is the actual person meant, and described here as 'Purujit of Kuntibhoja's kingdom'.

1:6
Subhadra's son, the sons of Draupadi. The son of Arjuna by Subhadra, and the sons of Arjuna and the other four Pandava brothers by Draupadi, to whom they were all simultaneously married.

1:7
O best among the twice born. Referring to Drona. The 'twice-born' is the common epithet for one who has received the sacred thread, his 'second' birth – a coming-of-age entitlement among the higher castes.

1:8
Bhishma is the respected elder statesman of the Kauravas and wise adviser to Dhritarashtra, whose role in the conflict about to unfold is considered pivotal by Duryodhana in his assessment of their chances. Among the legendary commanders whose names are recited here *Ashvatthama* is Drona's own son and *Vikarna* is the brother of Duryodhana.

1:10
Translators and commentators are divided as to whether the Kauravas are the stronger or weaker force, and this

verse is often given the opposite meaning. However, the apprehensiveness of Duryodhana that is already apparent is reinforced in 1:11 by his anxiety to protect Bhishma in the belief that skill in leadership will overcome strength in numbers.

Bhima, as Edgerton points out, is not the leader of the Pandava army but is introduced here for verbal effect. Lines two and four of this verse in Sanskrit have only the one consonantal difference, that between 'Bhima' and 'Bhishma'.

1:14
Krishna is here identified by one of his epithets, 'descendant of Madhu', and Arjuna as 'son of Pandu'.

1:15
wolflike. Literally, 'wolf-bellied', indicating both ferocity and appetite.

From this point onwards the epithets for Krishna become obscure and a little doubtful as to their literal translation. They are frequently used simply for verbal effect or as rhythmic components. I have left them from now on largely untranslated and unremarked, along with the historical names of the conch-shells and their divine attributes.

1:16
Nakula and Sahadeva. Two of the five Pandava brother-princes, who are twins, not previously mentioned by name.

1:17
Shikhandi is a son of Drupada (born a girl but miraculously transformed into a boy).

1:20
Arjuna is here identified by an epithet: 'the one who holds the banner with the design of the monkey' (the god Hanuman).

1:29
pale. This line is more often translated as 'my mouth dries up'. The noun here is *mukha*, which can mean both 'face' and 'mouth', described as 'drying up' or (blood) 'draining from'.

1:30
Gandiva. The name of Arjuna's bow, consistent with the epic tradition of associating the magical power of a name with the personal weapon of the hero. Like Siegfried's dragon-slaying sword Nothung, it is of divine making.

1:35
demon slayer. An epithet of Krishna. There are occasions, as here and in the following verse, where the choice of epithet is closely related to the action or its mood and adds to the drama.

heaven and earth. Literally, the 'three worlds' of mythology: the abode of the gods, the aether and the earth; or, in some accounts of this cosmology, heaven, earth and the subterranean regions.

1:36
Dhritarashtra's sons. The 'sons of Dhritarashtra' is the recurring rhetorical description of the Kauravas that, as we can see from the enumeration of the various kinships (only some of which I have represented in the translation) encompasses all the related combatants.

troubler of evil men. An epithet of Krishna, 'disturber' or 'tormenter' of (evil) men.

1:40

Verses 1:40 to 1:44 reflect both the deep psychological prohibition of transgressions against consanguinity by which the family, clan and tribe retain their place in the social order, and the duty of the powerful to sustain and defend the social order itself and their own privileges. The moral evil that these verses are concerned with is not the act of war itself, or killing or violence, or the justness or injustice of the causes of the conflict; it is rather the breaking of inviolable laws of social order leading to the corruption of caste divisions on which that order is founded. For the Aryan tribes in the early history of India, the purity of the bloodline and the stability of a society based on caste and caste duties was regarded, in theory at least, as an absolute order, as absolute in their minds as the covenant with the 'great Leviathan' that was, for Thomas Hobbes, the indisputable sovereign power without which society would descend into 'perpetuall warre of every man against his neighbour'.[1] The rules against unsuitable marriages and the prohibition of the remarriage of widows that would degrade the caste were codified, around the first century CE, in the law code of Manu, and it may be these injunctions that Arjuna is referring to when he speaks of having heard them 'time and time again'. These verses seek to locate the despondency of Arjuna in this moral transgression. Although this is the moral problem posed, it is not the moral problem developed and addressed in the opening verses of Book 2.

1:42

holy rites and offerings. The text literally reads, 'ritual offerings of rice balls and water', referring to the primitive vedic rites to sustain the welfare of the living and maintain the departed souls of the dead. Loss of status and neglect of rites are associated aberrations in the laws of Manu.

---

[1] Hobbes, Thomas. *Leviathan*. London, 1651. Chapter 20.

2

THE SELF, THE INDESTRUCTIBLE

Battles, the horrors of fratricidal wars, the fever of doubtful news,
*   the fitful events;*
These come to me days and nights and go from me again,
But they are not the Me myself. Walt Whitman, *Song of Myself*

2:1   And Krishna spoke to him,
        whose eyes were filled with tears
        and his heart with sorrow.

2:2   Why do you falter now,
        having come this far?
        It is not fitting
        to fall into disgrace
        and lose your place in heaven.

2:3   Weakness is no virtue.
        Arise! Stand up and fight!

2:4   And Arjuna replied:
        How can I raise my bow
        against my uncle, Bhima,
        or my master, Drona,
        whom rather I should venerate?

2:5   Better here on earth to beg for alms
        and eat a beggar's food
        than slay these noble minds
        and taste the fruits of my desires
        tainted by their blood.

2:6   We know not, facing Dhritarashtra's sons,
        which is the better way,

to win or lose,
if by their deaths
we should no longer wish to live.

2:7   My whole being is overcome
by pity, weakness and confusion.
Dispel my doubts and tell me
what my rightful duty is.

2:8   I truly cannot see an end to sorrow,
nor how kingship even of the earth
and over all the gods of heaven
could return me to my senses.

2:9   And Arjuna said:
I will not fight,
and having spoken thus
fell silent.

2:10   Then in this scene
between two armies in the field
where Arjuna silent and dejected sat,
Krishna smiled
and spoke these words:

*

2:11   You grieve for those
you need not mourn,
and though you seem
to speak with wisdom
you do not.
For the wise grieve
neither for the living
nor the dead.

2:12   In truth, there never was a time
when I was not,
and never will there be a time

when I shall cease to be,
nor a time for you,
nor for all these lords of men.

2:13   Through childhood, youth and age
I am, though all these pass.
Just so, my body passes on
and yet I am.
The wise know this.

2:14   Sensations come and go,
heat and cold,
pain or pleasure.
Endure them all,
they pass.

2:15   The wise man lets them go.
One for whom both
pain and pleasure are the same
conforms with his immortal self.

2:16   Nowhere will you find
not-being.
Being is all that can be found.
Know
that both these things
are true.

2:17   Know
the all-pervasive
cannot be destroyed,
that no one can destroy
the indestructible.

2:18   These bodies
gathered here

will meet their end.
And yet, I tell you,
there is that within
that has no end
and is not lost.
So fight this war!

2:19   If you think the self
the slayer
then you do not understand.
Do you think the self
is slain?
The self is neither
slayer nor the slain.

2:20   For neither is it born
nor will it die
nor having come to be
not be.
Unborn, indestructible,
endless and primordial,
it is not killed
when the body is slain.

2:21   For one who knows this,
that the self is unborn, indestructible,
how then can he be the slayer,
and who is killed?

2:22   These bodies
are like cast-off clothes.
We will find new ones.

2:23   Weapons cannot pierce
nor fire burn this.

It is not wetted by the waters,
nor withered by the wind.

2:24   It stands, eternal, everywhere,
immovable, unshakable,
primordial,

2:25   unmanifest, unthinkable,
unchanging.
Knowing this,
you have no cause to grieve.

2:26   Even if you think
it is the self that dies
to be eternally reborn,
you should not grieve,

2:27   for birth and death
are certain,
and you should not grieve.

2:28   First there is nothing,
then there is something,
then nothing again.
What complaint is there in this?

2:29   Some will see this as a wonder,
another tell it as a wonder
and yet another hear it as a wonder.
Yet, having heard it,
no one knows it,

2:30   this, the self,
the indestructible
that dwells in each of them.
And so you should not grieve
for anyone.

2:31   You should not waver

in your rightful duty.
A warrior has no greater cause
than righteous war.

2:32   And if your fortune
falls to you
the gates of heaven
will open.
This is your happy fate.

2:33   Sinfulness, not glory,
falls to one
who turns aside
from rightful conflict.

2:34   And people will forever speak
of your enduring shame.
Disgrace is worse than death
among the honourable.

2:35   Warriors who held you in regard
will slight you,
thinking you afraid.

2:36   Your enemies will scorn you
for your lack of will
with words that never should be said.
What is worse than this?

2:37   If you die
heaven is your reward,
and if you conquer
then this earth is yours.
Therefore stand up
and be resolved and fight.

2:38   Make pain and pleasure
       all the same to you,
       become indifferent
       to gains and losses,
       victory and defeat.
       Then join the fray
       and bring no blame
       upon yourself.

              *

2:39   Thus far have you heard
       the tenets of *samkhya*.
       Now hear
       how by the will
       and arduous practice
       you may escape
       the bonds of action.

2:40   A little effort,
       even, is not lost,
       nor does it lessen.
       A little is enough
       to save you from great danger.

2:41   In this there is but one
       resolute and insightful way.
       Their ways are numberless
       who lack it.

2:42   They love their flowery speech,
       delighted at their own interpretation
       of the words of law.
       And they will claim
       that there is nothing else.

2:43   These are men
whose minds are rooted in desire,
intent on heaven
and securing their rebirth,
meticulous in their performance of the rites
to bring them powers and pleasures.

2:44   Attached to pleasures
and their minds seduced like this,
they cannot have a single-minded understanding.

2:45   The rites belong to this world and its passions.
Release yourself from your desires,
learn to be indifferent to either/or
and fix your mind upon this single truth.
Free of self-interest and its possessions,
take possession of your self!

2:46   All the rites
have no more value
to the wise
than water in a well
when all the world
is full to overflowing.

2:47   Action alone is yours
and never its results.
Never let your motives
rule your actions,
yet neither let there be in you
attachment to inaction.

2:48   Abandoning attachment,
act single-mindedly
with equanimity,

which is, we say, the essence
of this discipline.

2:49   Actions in themselves
are far inferior to
determined understanding.
Discipline yourself
and find your refuge
in this wisdom.
Contemptible are they
who hope to gain
from everything they do.

2:50   In this world
the disciplined in mind
detach both good and evil
from their deeds.
Adopt this discipline in action
as the fitting way to act.

2:51   Wise men
firm in understanding
by abandoning the fruits
of all their actions
cast off the bonds
of life and death
and go beyond
the reach of pain.

2:52   When finally you've crossed
this quagmire of delusion
you'll be indifferent
to all that you have heard
and all that you will hear
concerning rites and sacrifices.

2:53   Disregard these doctrines
and let this inwardness
remain immovable,
quiescent and at peace,
and then this discipline
I speak of will be yours.

2:54   Tell me what this man is like,
firm in understanding,
centred in his being,
focused in his thoughts.
Tell me how he speaks
and sits and moves.

2:55   When he leaves behind
desires arising in the mind,
sufficient in himself
and self-contained:
then is he called
firm in understanding.

2:56   Not seeking happiness
and undisturbed by his misfortunes,
freed from anger, fear and passion,
focused in his thoughts:
then is he known as wise.

2:57   Desiring nothing,
everywhere he turns
he never turns to this
in preference to that,
pleasant or unpleasant:
then is he firm in wisdom.

2:58   Withdrawing all his senses
from the objects of the senses
like a turtle that withdraws
its limbs inside its shell:
then is he firm in wisdom.

2:59   The man who fasts
may turn aside from objects
of the senses
but the taste of them remains.
But he whose mind
is occupied with higher things
turns away from taste itself.

2:60   Yet even one who strives
for wisdom finds his mind
against his will
tormented and distracted
by the power of the senses.

2:61   Restraining them
and disciplined in mind
let him sit
intent on me
and rule his senses:
such a one is firm in wisdom.

2:62   Focusing on objects of the senses
breeds attachment
and then attachment leads to
wanting them and wanting
them to anger and frustration

2:63   and confusion of the mind.
Then we forget
and wander,
and wandering

lose sight of wisdom,
and without wisdom
we are lost.

2:64   But he who has detached himself
from all desires and hates,
even though he moves
among the objects of the senses
governs them with self-control,
and so finds peace of mind.

2:65   With tranquil mind
all sorrows cease,
and from tranquillity
comes all at once
that understanding
that is firm and true.

2:66   There is no understanding
without the discipline of self-control
and no attempt at it
without determined effort,
and where there is no effort
nor is there abiding peace of mind.
And how can anyone be happy
unquiet in his mind?

2:67   When the mind is guided
by the senses, the understanding
wanders like a ship
blown by the roaming wind
across the waters.

2:68   Only he who has withdrawn his senses
from the objects of the senses
can be firm in wisdom.

2:69   His wakefulness
is night for other beings
whose day is night to him.
And so it is
for one who wakes and sees.

2:70   Just so, the one who lets
desires enter and dissolve
in him unmoved, as seas
absorb the flowing stream,
will find tranquillity of mind –
not so for one
always desirous of desires.

2:71   The man who frees himself
from all desires, lusts and longing,
and lives indifferent
to 'me' and 'mine',
finds peace.

2:72   There is a holy state
free from all delusions
that even at the hour of death
a man may reach.

NOTES ON THE TEXT AND TRANSLATION

The first ten verses of Book 2 are a continuation of the epic setting and an extension of the moral problem that has led to Arjuna's despondency. But the cause of his moral conflict has now subtly shifted from transgressions of the laws of caste and family to a more general sense of guilt and irresolution. Arjuna's question now relates to his 'duty' (*dharma*), and Krishna's response and his exhortations remain firmly within the bounds of the *kshatriya* warrior code of honour. The question now becomes: 'Given that one's duty is inescapable, action unavoidable and death inevitable, how should I act and still retain the moral integrity I see in not acting?' The answer lies in understanding who it is who acts, and the discovery of the still and immovable integrity of the self within, around which action revolves but which does not itself act.

The moral teaching commences with verse 2:11. Verses 2:11 to 2:30 are concerned with the indestructibility and deathlessness of the self and its indifference to the destruction of the body, which is no more to be mourned than the passage from childhood to age. The section from 2:31 to 2:38 picks up the theme of *kshatriya* caste duty begun in 2:2 and 2:3. The argument of these verses remains within a materialistic frame of reference, the 'you' addressed being throughout the fated one who may go to heaven or inherit power and wealth on earth. That 'you' is not the indestructible 'embodied self' untouched by its actions. This immovable, unaffected, uninvolved self 'permits' the action to which it is indifferent, signified in 2:38: 'Then you may fight and bring no blame upon yourself'. The process of acquiring what might be summarised as the 'wisdom of the self' is the theme of the verse sequence from 2:39 onwards, in which the self's freedom from the bonds of action is declared, pointing the way to the practical discipline (*yoga*) required to achieve a state of inner equanimity and tranquillity.

I have excluded from the text as unnecessarily intrusive the occasional references to Sanjaya, the ostensible narrator, and Dhritarashtra, to whom, at the beginning, the tale is being told. I have also from now on omitted the several epithets for both Arjuna and Krishna, which are often used as rhythmic line fillers. I have passed over in silence, in common with many other translators, 'O thick-haired one', 'O bristling-haired one', 'Scourge of the enemy' and 'Chief cow herder'.

2:2
having come this far. 'having arrived at this misfortune, at this point of danger'. Having arrived at this point of crisis, it is too late to avoid the inescapable consequences of actions previously taken, motivated by ambition for wealth and power, and the drama must inexorably be played out. It is cowardice not simply to refuse to fight, but to refuse to see through to the bitter end the train of events you set in motion by the decisions you made and the actions you took in the past. How to bear the inevitable by separating the inner self in its stillness from the outward self and its actions is the theme of the teaching from 2:11 onwards.

It is not fitting. 'It is unAryan'.

heaven. In mythology, the place to which the soul departs to await its rebirth.

2:4
raise my bow. 'attack with arrows'.

2:5
here on earth. Arjuna's immediate concern is not with his place in heaven but his duty here on earth, proposing to sacrifice the tainted taste of his fulfilled ambitions for a religious supplicant's sufficiency.

2:7

tell me. It is at this point that Arjuna surrenders his will to Krishna and thereby establishes the master/pupil relationship that allows the discourse that follows to unfold.

2:13

We are accustomed to the passing of these 'ages of man' without distress:

> *Growing is the strange death*
> *In life that nobody mourns* [1]

2:19

Verses 2:19 and 2:20 are taken from verses 2:18 and 2:19 of the *Katha Upanishad*, the source also for the opening verse of Emerson's poem, *Brahma*:

> *If the red slayer think he slays,*
> *Or if the slain think he is slain,*
> *They know not well the subtle ways*
> *I keep, and pass, and turn again.*

2:22

We should avoid reading into this verse a doctrine of the transmigration of the soul. What is being described here, taken with the preceding verse, is the transitory nature of the phenomenal world in which bodies and their sensations come and go, which is also the world in which actions take place, and, antithetically, the indestructible, imperishable transcendent nature of the self, beyond action, for whom they are merely phenomena.

---

[1] Smart, Elizabeth. *Babies in A Bonus*. London, Polytantric Press, 1977.

2:23
this. The embodied self.

2:26
Even if you think. Even if you do not immediately grasp the transcendent nature of the self, and take the conventional view of the cycle of birth and death, reason tells you that we have no knowledge of the time before our coming into being nor of the time when we cease to exist. We can know only our being. This is the common reasoning of those reflections on death that rationally exclude a belief in immortality or an afterlife, such as the assertion of Lucretius: 'Death is nothing to us'.[1]

2:31
rightful duty and *righteous war*. Both phrases employ the term *dharma*.

2:32
'If it is your fate to die you will enter heaven, a happy estate reserved for the noble fallen.'

2:38
This verse acts as a bridge from the premise of the indestructibility of the embodied self and its equanimity towards the destruction of the body to the doctrine of the self's detachment from its actions (and in particular from ritual actions that serve some end result) and thereby from guilt, blame or 'evil'.

2:39
This declaration of the subject of the discourse that follows introduces several new concepts and terms that need some elucidation.

---

[1] Lucretius, *De rerum natura*, 3:830

Thus far have you heard the tenets of samkhya. The *samkhya* was one of the main influential Indian schools of philosophy and is usually regarded as the speculative body of philosophy of which *yoga* is the more practical arm. Krishna here speaks both as an exponent of that philosophy and as a *yogin*, and will continue to teach elements of *samkhya* throughout the *Gita*. The *samkhya* is a rational or (in its literal translation) 'enumerative' philosophy. It does in fact attempt to systematise hierarchically and numerically the elements of being and knowing from the top level duality of cosmic spirit and matter through their downward evolution as conscious intelligence and then human individuation as the ego in possession of mind and the sense organs, through the combination of which a person is able to understand the formal nature of the world and act in it. There is no dependency on 'God' in this philosophy, which rejects both the vedic sacrifice and extreme forms of ascetic practice, teaching release from suffering through the renunciation of desire and the self's attachment to 'me' and 'mine'.

the will. Another concept is introduced here, *buddhi*, commonly translated as 'intelligence' – which will serve in most contexts. But it carries more weight than 'intelligence' or 'intellect'. Zaehner[1] reads the first line of 2:41 as 'the essence of *buddhi* is will'; that is, 'self-will'. In order to avoid confusion between the various ways we loosely describe the self in natural and non-technical language, *buddhi* might best be defined as the 'intelligent awakened will'. *Buddhi*, as a further concept of 'self', helps to describe the common human experience of the awakening of the will lying dormant in the 'ego'-self that is absorbed in its own interests, tied to its wants and needs until some crisis precipitates a revaluation of its values. (When we say: 'I' am determined to

---

[1] Zaehner, R. C. *Hindu Scriptures.* Everyman's Library, 1992.

get 'myself' out of this situation, we are clearly in possession of two different ideas of the self.) In this part of the *Gita*, that situation is typified in the person of Arjuna, who until this 'point of crisis' has been motivated by the attachments of the self (ego) to ambition, wealth and power. Now, having awakened to the consequences of his ego-driven actions, he is being exhorted to apply himself (*buddhi*) to the determined practice (*yoga*) of releasing himself from those attachments in order to awaken the enduring self (*dehi* or *atman*) within. So we have here three ideas of the self: the ego at the beginning, the enlightened 'self' at the end, and the 'determined will' of the self as the practical bridge between them.

by...arduous practice. 'in *yoga*'.

the bonds of action. This is the first occurrence of the word *karma*, meaning 'action', the dominant theme of the *Gita*. It is less the subject of this sentence than 'bonds'. The bonds are the moral entanglements attached to actions driven by the passions of self-interest and the ego's attachment to its aims and interests, wishes and desires. What our actions bind us to is the endless wheel of life, death and rebirth. Freedom lies in the realisation of the self which does not act, is unattached to its actions. Arjuna is urged to act in this battle in selfless submission to the *dharma* of the *kshatriya* warrior. No one, in fact, will act. The action will simply unfold. The verses that follow go on to excoriate the performance of ritual actions as a deluded way of liberation, for release is not to be gained through any actions to whose results we remain attached, but only by detachment achieved through determined effort and self-discipline.

2:40

great danger. A danger that lies in continuing to believe that by performing 'right' actions in accordance with the vedic rites you will receive the rewards you seek. Even a little effort will set you on the right path to a singular understanding and lead you away from the multiple ritual practices that only further enmesh you in attachments to the fruits of your actions. This becomes clearer in the following verses that launch an attack on the insufficiency of vedic rites, sacrifices and incantations to be the last word in wisdom.

2:42

In the *samkhya* philosophy there are no gods, and it dismisses the effectiveness of rites and sacrifices, which of course is anathema to the Brahmins whose self-esteem is founded on their skill at elaborate commentary and interpretation, and who vigorously defend the necessity of their intervention in every aspect of the conduct of daily life. The Brahmins inhabited a parallel world of words, for whom, said Chaudhuri, 'the universe became a space-time-word continuum, instead of being only a space-time continuum'.[1]

2:43

rebirth as the fruit of their (ritual) actions. This part of the verse is often mistranslated with the meaning, 'condemned by their actions to endless rebirth', but the meaning here is 'seeking rebirth in a higher form as the just deserts for their (correctly carried out) ritual actions'. 'Those who do not understand' are mired in the world of desires and attachments, as the following two verses will make clear in consigning the vedic rites to the realm of the gross passions of mind and body in contrast to this teaching of 'single-minded understanding' (*buddhi*).

2:45

The rites belong to this world and its passions. The literal

---

[1] Chaudhuri, Nirad C. *Hinduism*. London: Chatto & Windus, 1979. p.217

translation is: 'The Vedas belong in the category (to the world) of the three *gunas*'. The three *gunas* are the temperaments of the personality whose admixture of light and dark, good and bad impulses, makes up the character and characteristic behaviour of the individual. And 'a man's character,' to quote Heraclitus, 'is his *daimon*.' The *gunas* are referred to throughout the *Gita* (and explained more fully in the Note to 7:12). They represent the individual (uncontrolled) will – the will to power and the will to live – untempered by the subjective will (*buddhi*), which requires an understanding of the true nature of the self before the *gunas* can be transcended. The *gunas* are associated with the passions, with worldly attachments, the pursuit of wealth, power and pleasure, and the satisfaction of the desires of self-interest – however those interests manifest themselves in the personality between the two extremes of relentless ambition and fatalistic surrender. Adherence to the rites is assigned to the motivations of the *gunas*. It is in the nature of man to seek out gods in order to gain power and the objects of his desires. The role of the *gunas* in ritual worship is taken up again in 7:20, and at length in Book 17.

either/or. The opposites, heat and cold, pain and pleasure.

this single truth. '*sattva*' in Sanskrit. Since *sattva* is also the Sanskrit word for the nobler of the three *gunas*, its use here has occasionally led to some confusion. If it is taken to refer to the *sattvic guna*, then the verse would mean: 'free yourself from all three *gunas* and then fix your mind firmly on one', which is nonsensical in this context; and, in any case, the *gunas* are not separable but are seen as interwoven strands of the individual temperament. The 'single truth' is the resolute insight of 2:41.

your self. '*atman*', here introduced for the first time. Up to this point *dehi* has been employed as the term for the 'embodied self', the endlessness within.

2:46

the wise. 'the wise Brahmin who understands' and not the wise man in general is the stricter reading of this line. That specific usage would logically be required in this context since the Vedas are the preserve of the Brahmins. The connotation here is that the wise man has all he needs when he realises that the self fills the whole cosmos. The wisdom of the Vedas is a drop in the ocean of the wisdom of the self.

2:47

The only permitted actions are necessary actions, duty. All other actions are motivated by the good (fortune) they will bring (continuing to implicate the Vedas in this). In the theory of the *gunas*, the active personality (*rajas*) is governed by his desire for success, and the inactive (*tamas*) by a lack of motivation – the dark side of the personality, indifferent to or unaware of right and duty. You should not be attached to motives and results, but neither must you fail to do what you *must* do. The injunction against inaction occurs here partly for deliberate antithesis, but also, perhaps, to pre-empt the thought that if I am to detach myself from my motives to act, the easiest way to do this is not to act at all. And that, in fact, is the question that will open the dialogue in Book 3.

2:48

attachment. By which is meant attachment to the fruits or results of actions.

single-mindedly. 'fixed in, abiding in *yoga*'.

we say. 'it is said', 'it is said (in this teaching) that this equanimity of mind is *yoga*'.

2:49

Actions in themselves are far inferior to determined understanding.
'Action (*karma*, of the motivated kind previously referred to,
including the performance of the vedic rites) is far inferior
to this disciplined understanding (*buddhi-yoga*)'. It becomes
clear, here and in verses 2:52 and 2:53 that follow, that by the
'fruits of action' the teaching implicates ritual practices (also
called '*karma*') for motivated ends and does not just refer to
motivated actions in general.

2:50

discipline in action. The last two lines effectively define *karma-
yoga* as the right way to live by reconciling the two imperatives
to understand and to act, whose apparent contradiction will
be explored further in the early part of Book 3.

2:52

indifferent to. Or 'dismissive of'.

2:53

this discipline I speak of will be yours. I have added 'I speak of'
to link this conclusive line to all that has been taught so far
about the way of *yoga* in contrast to the way of the Vedas, and
to make it clear that what is 'obtained' here (the text is 'you
will obtain *yoga*') is (proficiency in) the practical discipline
(*yoga*) itself and not some other resultant state of mind ('self-
realisation' in Sargeant's translation, 'state of perfect *yoga*'
in Easwaran's, and even 'divine consciousness' in one of the
many Hindu interpretations.[1]

2:54

This verse, given to Arjuna, acts simply as an invitation to
continue the description of the qualities of one who adheres

---

[1] *Bhagavad-gita As It Is.* The Bhaktivedanta Book Trust, 1977.

to the *yoga* teaching. While not directly responding to the latter part of the question, Krishna, as teacher, lays the ground for addressing the problem of reconciling action with inner stillness. What follows continually reiterates what has been said before on detachment from desire and the world of the senses in order to achieve a state of inner strength and peace. It can all be understood outside the formal practice of meditation, but some elements of the answer, and the word 'sit' in the question itself, clearly suggest that some of these passages relate to the disciplined practice and postures of concentration and meditation, more evidently from 2:61 onwards.

2:59

The meditative practice of stilling the mind is here contrasted with contemporary austere practices of fasting and self-mortification as a way of subduing the senses. Both *yoga* and Buddhist meditation, one realising the self, the other annihilating the self, were opposed to these mendicant practices.

2:60

tormented and distracted. There are two subtly different inferences here. Desires stimulated by the senses continue to arise to torment you; attention to sensory objects distracts the mind from its internal focus in meditation. This latter meaning is carried forward into the next verse. The Stoic Seneca said in this regard: 'No trifle, mark you, to combine human frailty with divine tranquillity.'[1]

2:61

let him sit intent on me. This is the first use in the text of 'me'

---

[1] *Seneca's Letters to Lucilius*, translated by E. Phillips Barker. Oxford: Clarendon Press, 1932. (53).

as an object of attention. There is no reason to read into this line, at this stage of the guidance on stilling the mind given by teacher to pupil, an equation of 'me' with anything or anyone other than the self. The 'me' here is the inner controlled self, contrasted with the attention in meditation to objects of the senses given in the following verse. In plain English we might say 'intent on the me'. The 'me' is the 'me' of Walt Whitman's line: 'To me the converging objects of the universe perpetually flow'.[1] Later, Krishna as teacher will increasingly speak on behalf of and *as* the self, the self without limits.

2:63

wisdom. 'buddhi' – the willed, enlightened intelligence, the seat of wisdom.

2:66

determined effort. 'bhavana'. This word has been subject to many and varied interpretations. If we believe that this verse is discussing the practice of meditation then 'concentration' may be a reasonable interpretation, though Zaehner thinks this wrong. Edgerton has 'efficient-force', and I have taken my lead from him in believing that the intention here is to draw a distinction between the controlled and uncontrolled mind, and to reiterate the need for the willed action of *buddhi* to make a disciplined effort to achieve that control. Some of the difficulty arises from the concision of the original and its playful antithesis. The meaning is: 'There is no will in the undisciplined mind to bring it under control, and without the discipline to bring it under control no peace of mind can be achieved.'

---

[1] *Song of Myself.* (line 404).

2:72

a holy state. The text refers to *'brahma-nirvana'*, the extinguishing of the self in *brahman*. This seems to have been a conscious attempt to associate the goal of detachment with Buddhist *nirvana*. But there is nothing elsewhere in the *Gita* that approaches the more rigorous Buddhist teaching on the illusory nature of the self or its final abnegation in *nirvana*. The tranquil state of mind described in this chapter has much more in common with the *apatheia* of the Stoics and the *ataraxia* of the Sceptics of the Pyrrhonist school.[1]

even at the hour of death. The closing verse of this chapter is widely misinterpreted. It is often understood to represent the transition to a new order of being at the point of death, a passing 'from death to immortality'.[2] The keyword here is 'even'. It is not too late, even at the hour of death, to free oneself from delusion and achieve *nirvana* – the Buddhist term for the extinguishing of the ego-self and its attachments, self-interests and passions.

---

[1] See: Zeller, E. *The Stoics, Epicureans and Sceptics.* London: Longmans, Green, and Co., 1892.

[2] Easwaran, 2007.

3

THE WAY OF ACTION

*I also say it is good to fall, battles are lost in the same spirit
in which they are won.* Walt Whitman, *Song of Myself*

3:1   If you think
awakening the understanding
is superior to action
then why do you commit me
to this most terrible of deeds?

3:2   Your words
confuse my understanding
by seeming to possess two meanings.
Tell me what the one way is
that would be right to follow.

3:3   Two ways have I taught
since ancient times.
One way is the way of wisdom
known to the philosophers,
the other is the way of action
followed by the disciplined in mind.

3:4   Man does not free himself
from action
by not acting,
nor by relinquishing the world
pass beyond it.

3:5   Never for a moment
can we live and yet not act.
Everyone must act to live.
We act and live
against our will,
for nature wills it.

3:6   He who sits
attempting to restrain his impulses to act
while thinking of the objects of the senses
just deludes himself.
We call this man unnatural.

3:7   But he who undertakes
the subjugation of the senses
with his mind
and acts without attachment
to his impulses to act
we call superior.

3:8   Act! Do what must be done.
Action is superior to non-action.
Simply to survive
you need to act!

3:9   This world is such
that action cannot be avoided.
The only action that is free
is worship.
Do this freely.

*

3:10   He who is creator
of the world

created man
together with the sacrifice
and said:
By sacrifices may you have
all that you desire.

3:11   By nourishing the gods
the gods will nurture you
and bring about
your greatest happiness.

3:12   Nourished by your offerings
the gods will grant you
all your pleasures,
but he who takes his pleasures
without sacrifices
is no better than a thief.

3:13   Good men of faith
who eat the food
remaining from the sacrifice
are blessed,
but those who eat it
for their own sake
consume their wickedness.

3:14   For food is the beginning
of existence,
and rain its source,
and the god who sends the rain
comes into being himself
through acts of sacrifice.

3:15   The rites and offerings
were given in the Vedas
which themselves derive
from the imperishable.
Thus all-pervading *brahman*
is eternalised by sacrifice.

3:16   The wheel is set in motion

and he who does not turn with it
lives a wicked life of useless sensuality.

*

3:17   He who is entirely
self-contained,
contented in the self
and needing nothing else,
has no need to act.

3:18   He seeks nothing
by his actions
and nothing by not acting
and has no need
of anyone
for anything.

3:19   In all your actions
do what must be done
but act without attachment.
To act without attachment
is to reach man's highest state of being.

3:20   Look to Janaka and his like
who found perfection
acting in the world.
And seeing how the world
itself coheres through action,
you should act.

3:21   The world follows
where the best men lead.

3:22   For me
there is nothing

in this world
that I must do
and nothing lacking
to be sought.
And yet I act.

3:23   Were I not untiringly
to act
all men would follow
where I lead,

3:24   the world would perish
in confusion
and I would be the cause
of their destruction.

3:25   The unwise act
with motives for their actions.
The wise act simply
to sustain the order of the world.

3:26   And yet one should not disillusion
those who have no wisdom.
The wise man leaves them
to enjoy the actions
they are tied to
and ties himself to selfless action.

3:27   Every action in this world
is governed by the will
at work in nature.
The self deludes itself
in thinking that it acts.

3:28   But he who knows the truth
that actions are the work
of that which acts upon itself

does not attach himself to them.

3:29   The one who knows
        should not disturb the mind
        of one who does not know
        his actions are not his to own.

3:30   Surrender all your acts to me.
        Ask for nothing, wish for nothing.
        Mindful only of the supreme self,
        with equanimity and free
        from all desire for what is yours,
        fight!
        and let your fever
        and your grief depart.

        *

3:31   Those who speak no ill
        of it but follow faithfully
        my doctrine
        are liberated from
        the bonds of action.

3:32   But know this –
        those who do not follow it
        and murmur at my doctrine
        are lost,
        stupid, and confused
        about the nature of all wisdom.

3:33   All material beings
        follow their material nature
        when they act –
        the wise man too.

What point is there
in trying to subdue it?

3:34   But yet you must not
give control to these two
brigands of the highway,
the passions of desire and hate
arising in the senses
from the objects of the senses.

3:35   Better your own duty,
though imperfect,
than another's duty well-performed.
Better death in your own calling
than inviting harm by undertaking
duties that belong to others.

　　　*

3:36   What is it that compels
a man to evil deeds
against his will,
as though another's will
commanded him?

3:37   The forces of desire and anger
are commanded by the great
and all-consuming evil
of the will to power.
This is your antagonist.

3:38   As fire is hidden
by the smoke,
the glass by dust,

the embryo concealed
within the membrane,
3:39   so the wisdom of the wise
is clouded by desire,
that eternal enemy,
unquenchable as fire.

3:40   For know the enemy
has taken up position in the senses,
in the mind and in the will,
obscuring wisdom
and deluding the embodied self within.

3:41   First, bring your senses
under your control,
then strike this demon,
destroyer of all wisdom
and right judgment.

3:42   They say the senses are superior,
the mind higher.
Intelligence is higher still.
Above them all stands
this!

3:43   and therefore, knowing
this – the higher self –
by the self uphold the self,
destroy your enemy
whose shifting shape
takes on the form of all desires,
so hard to meet with
and so hard to conquer.

NOTES ON THE TEXT AND TRANSLATION

Arjuna's request in 2:54, 'Tell me what this man is like', has led on to a deeper development of the theme of realising the inner self 'firm in understanding', latterly through disciplined practice and focused meditation. We appear to be heading towards a doctrine of renunciation which might appear to have lost sight of the imperative to act without attachment which had been the subject of the discourse up to this point. Arjuna's understandable confusion at this juncture allows Krishna to return to that theme and make it clear that, on both an earthly and a cosmic scale, action is both necessary and unavoidable, and in 3:30 to conclude the argument with a further injunction to fight in the battle: 'Fight, and let your fever and your grief depart'.

A man acts because he must, and because it is his duty. The man of *karma-yoga*, firmly at one with himself at the centre of his being, understands that he himself does not act. Something else acts for him, the *gunas*, the wilful forces of his material nature. He is free even from the performance of the vedic rites which, as we have learned (2:45), belong to the world of the *gunas* because they are performed with expectations or, in some cases, with evil intent towards others to secure power and advantage for oneself. The only truly free acts the self can perform are acts of devotion, acts of sacrifice performed without attachment.

Book 3 ends with Krishna's exhortation to recognise the 'higher', detached self and to do battle with the temptations of the senses.

3:1
awakening the understanding. 'buddhi'.

3:3
Two ways have I taught since ancient times. The *jnana-yoga*

of the *samkhya* school and *karma-yoga*. By attributing both
teachings – the wisdom of insight and insightful wisdom
as the basis of right action – to his own person, Krishna
establishes both the timelessness of the teaching and the
recurrence of the teacher over historical time as a necessary
fact. See 4:7-8 where that personal recurrence and its
necessity are definitively expressed.

the way of wisdom known to the philosophers. 'jnana (knowledge/
wisdom) *yoga* of the *samkhyas'*. This is the way (*yoga*) of
the followers of the *samkhya* contemplative school of self-
realisation detached from the world of action.

the way of action followed by the disciplined in mind. 'karma-yoga
of the *yogins'*. This is the way of the *yogins*, followers of the
yoga school of self-realisation in action. The *yogins* have of
course acquired the wisdom (*jnana*) of the *samkhya* school but
are able to reconcile that understanding with the continuing
need to act in the world. See verse 2:50.

3:5
nature wills it. 'it is willed by the *gunas* born of material
nature'. The *gunas*, the will in nature, cause us to act, even
against our own will, since our being originates in material
nature (*prakriti*) and is indivisible from it.

3:6
He who sits. This verse refers to the austere practices of those
'philosophers' who have cast off the bonds of action in the
world and who attempt to reach the highest goal by subduing
their natural and even physiological impulses. In contrast,
3:7 describes the follower of *karma-yoga* practice.

3:9
Do this freely. 'free from attachment (to ends and motives)'.

Throughout this teaching on the theme of action and non-action, *karma* has meant both action as the fulfilment of duty or necessity and action as ritual action, and in both cases the text has contrasted actions performed in the pursuit of ends and rewards with actions unattached to their fruits, actions that do not contain the 'self' as the actor/agent of the act. It is this important distinction in relation to ritual acts, offerings and sacrifices that is now being made, doubly important for the way in which it will later be developed into an all-embracing idea of devotion (*bhakti*).

The actions that can't be helped are those actions of the natural will tied to the nature of matter, mind and the maintenance of the natural order of the world. As such, none of those acts are free, but of necessity must be undertaken if we are to live, and live in any ordered fashion. The point will also be made in ensuing verses that the social fabric endures through the performance of equally necessary acts of duty or *dharma*. It is, in this theory, the *gunas* that provide both the conscious and unconscious motive power for actions that seek the ends of self-interest. Through the discipline being promoted here the self detaches itself from those actions and *does not itself act*. The untied, boundless self takes no part in these actions. Free from this bondage, turning away from all attachments, the self has this one unattached freedom to act: to choose the act of devotion. In the deeper religious sense we turn to God *because* it is not a necessary act.

W H Auden has drawn out that same distinction, in relation to what he calls the 'aesthetic religion' of the Greeks, in which the gods are the embodiment of the passions that drive action: 'The Greeks and the Trojans must fight because "hateful Ares bids". To the aesthetic religion all act is ritual, acts designed to attract the divine favours which will make the self strong, and ritual is the only form of activity in which man has the freedom to act or refrain from acting and for which, therefore, he is responsible.'[1]

The disquisition that follows in 3:10-16 seems to state the brahmanic position on the centrality of ritual, triggered by the thought in 3:9. However, the explanation of the relationship between man and God (or gods) established at the creation for the maintenance of the created helps to propel the argument forward to the Veda-less conclusion in 3:17-18, picking up the train of thought again in 3:19 – that the self needs nothing other than the self (*atman*), which in the *Gita* is cognate with *brahman*.

3:10

He who is creator. 'Prajapati' in the text, the 'creator' god who in mythology sacrificed himself to become the food of the gods. God himself is the original sacrifice. This idea leads to the logic of 3:15 that therefore *brahman* is established in the sacrifice from the beginning: that is, *brahman* is also subject to the ministrations of the Brahmins.

3:15

This is a piece of brahmanic logic to show that 'all-pervading *brahman*' is subject to the vedic ritual, since both the Vedas and *brahman* are deemed to have arisen at once, in this argument, from the same imperishable source. Yet the primitive myth of the original sacrifice in 3:10 hides a profound psychological truth: that God is born of sacrifice and sustained by acts of homage, the deep-rooted origin of the doctrine of devotion developed later in the *Gita*.

3:16

The wheel is set in motion. The sacrifices create an endless cycle of interdependence. Those who step outside it, who do not conform to what has been ordained, are here disparaged as wicked, sensual and without purpose.

[1] Kierkegaard, Søren, and W. H. Auden. *Kierkegaard, Selected and Introduced by W. H. Auden.* London: Cassell, 1955.

3:17

has no need to act. Has no need to perform the rites. He has already sacrificed the fruits of action to the self and gained all that can be desired in this world.

3:20

Janaka. It is reasonable to believe that this Janaka is the philosopher-king of the *Brihadaranyaka Upanishad* who was also, like Arjuna, of the *kshatrya* caste. There appears to be a suggestion here, in continuing to urge Arjuna to fight in this battle, that the performance of caste duty is essential to maintaining the order of the world. But the overall direction of the verse is to show that the wisdom of the self is consistent with examples of the most rigorous forms of dutiful action, kingship and state administration, leading the argument into the next two important verses.

3:22

For me. Here, for the first time, Krishna speaks as the personification of *brahman*, the impersonal sustaining imperative of universal order.

3:23

all men would follow where I lead. The argument is not entirely logical. The line is there to complement, poetically, 3:21: 'The world follows where the best men lead.' The point, however, is that if the sustaining principle of the world ceased to act it would bring about the destruction of all living creatures (3:24), and, similarly, the social order would be destroyed if men neglected to perform their *dharma* or caste duty by which that order is maintained.

3:25

with motives for their actions. 'attached to (the object of) action'.

3:26

The Vedas and the observance of the rites seem to be implicated again here. Those still attached to their actions should not be discouraged, for at least they are performing them, and there is a danger of putting doubts in their minds by challenging their ignorance with one's (higher) wisdom and leading them to inaction. One's duty is to perform one's own actions in the light of the *yoga* discipline (as the one thing an individual can truly effect) and, we may presume, become that exemplary man that others will follow (3:21).

3:27

the will at work in nature. The *gunas*.

3:28

that acts upon itself. The *gunas* are ascribed a twofold role as that which acts and that which is acted upon, the motivating force and the motivation. The intention is to describe a self-sufficient process in which the idea of the self as agent is simply an illusion. Here, 'attached' relates not to the 'fruits' of actions but to actions themselves erroneously understood as the work of the self as agent.

3:30

Surrender all your acts to me. Act without acting yourself. Again, Krishna speaks as the universal imperative, the originator of the *gunas* (see 7:12) and the impersonal force through which all deeds and works are accomplished. This verse marks a natural conclusion by returning us to Arjuna's state of mind in the midst the battle.

3:31

The next three verses offer some evidence of the doctrinal disputes that are taken up in the *Gita*. The brahmanic context and the disputed ground of belief, understanding

and practice have become evident in the *Gita's* challenges
to the performance of the vedic rites, its opposition to
ascetic practices and to the *samkhya* school itself insofar as
it teaches withdrawal from the world of action. The *karma-
yoga* discipline promoted in the *Gita* elevates the wisdom of
the self above all other teachings and practices. Its dispute
is with the Brahmins and the *pandits*, not with ordinary folk
(see 3:26 and 3:29) who can be left in peace.

3:34
brigands of the highway. The 'two enemies' or 'two obstacles'
along the way, the two overriding passions of attraction and
repulsion, likes and dislikes (based on Zaehner's reading).

3:35
inviting harm. 'inviting danger' – the danger of disrupting
caste duty and the coherence of the caste system by
crossing boundaries. There is little to justify the presence
of this loosely connected verse, duplicated almost word for
word from verse 18:47, where the subject is treated more
extensively.

3:36
The question is given to Arjuna, and follows not from 3:35
but from 3:34. It allows Krishna to continue the explanation
of the actions of the *gunas*, the source of the passions of anger
and desire and of the two 'enemies', attraction and repulsion,
identified in 3:34.

3:37
the will to power. The objectified will of the *rajas guna*, the
angry, power-seeking, aggressive, self-aggrandising, fiery
element of the driven ego. Amiel noted in his *Journal Intime*
that 'for action nothing is more useful than narrowness of

mind joined to energy of will.'[1]

3:40

For know. 'It is said' – in the *samkhya* philosophy, that part of it that deals with the descent from primal matter of the mind, the senses and the discriminating intelligence.

3:41

right judgment. 'vijnana'.

3:42

They say. 'They say (in the *samkhya* theory)'. The senses, in the hierarchy of evolution, are said to be superior to the gross elements of material being.

intelligence. 'buddhi'.

this! The self, identified in 3:43. The same passage occurs in the *Katha Upanishad* at 3:10, where the final line reads: 'Higher than intelligence is the great self'.

3:43

by the self uphold the self. Knowing the higher self, you should use this insight to keep the (lower) self under control and confront its temptations. See 6:5 for a parallel.

[1] Amiel, Henri Frédéric. *The Private Journal of Henri Frédéric Amiel*, translated by Van Wyck Brooks and Charles Van Wyck Brooks. New York: Macmillan, 1935. (Journal entry for May 31, 1880).

4

THE FIRE OF WISDOM

Why should I pray? why should I venerate and be ceremonious?
Walt Whitman, *Song of Myself*

4:1   This changeless way
        I first declared
        to Vivasvat and he
        transmitted it to Manu
        and Manu to Ikshvaku,
4:2   descending by succession
        through the royal line of seers.
        But over time it has been lost.
4:3   Now I declare to you
        this supreme secret,
        for you are my devoted friend.

4:4   How am I to understand
        that you declared this
        when the world began,
        before you had been born?

4:5   We both have passed
        through many births.
        I know them all
        though you do not.
4:6   For I am that
        imperishable unborn self,
        the lord of being,

that manifests itself
by its own power
in this material world.

4:7   Whenever righteousness
is in decline and in its place
unrighteousness arises
then do I once more arise.

4:8   I am born again in every age
to re-establish righteousness.
I am a haven for the virtuous,
I am the nemesis of the wicked.

4:9   He who knows in truth
my actions and my birth
are both divine
is not reborn
when he departs his body.
He comes to me.

4:10   Many are they who come to me,
abandoning their fear
and greed and anger,
and cleansed by hard-won wisdom
come to be as I am.

4:11   Follow my path.
However they may
come to me
I am their reward.

4:12   Those who only want
instant success
will surely get that
worshipping their gods
with ritual acts of sacrifice.

4:13   I am the source
of order in the world,
determined by the will in nature.
Yet though I have created this
I do nothing of myself
through all eternity.

4:14   Actions do not touch me,
nor do I desire anything
arising from them.
He who fully comprehends me
is just as free.

4:15   In ancient times
we knew this
and those who sought
their freedom
acted in the light of it.
Act, as they did.

4:16   What is meant by action
and non-action?
Even poets of old
were easily confused in this.
I will explain,
and when you understand
you will be free.

4:17   The way of action
is difficult to comprehend.
One must learn
what action is
and what wrong action is
and what non-action is.

4:18   One disciplined in wisdom
acts
but learns to see
non-action
in his actions
and in not acting
action.

4:19   Enlightened ones
will call him wise
who rids himself
of all desires and hopes
in everything he does,
consuming all his actions
in the fire of wisdom.

4:20   He who has abandoned
all attachment to any expectations
from his actions,
content within himself
with no dependency
on anyone for anything,
when he acts
in fact does nothing.

4:21   His mind controlled,
indifferent to wanting,
hoping, grasping, getting,
when he acts his body merely
acts the part for him.
He himself incurs no fault.

4:22   When whatever comes his way
contents him,
preferring neither

this nor that,
free from envy,
caring nothing for success
or failure,
then he is not bound
by any of his actions.

4:23   One whose mind
is firm in wisdom,
free from all attachments,
is released
and all his actions vanish
in the act of sacrifice.

*

4:24   For the offering is *brahman*
and the oblation is *brahman*
and the fire and the pouring
out into the fire are also *brahman*
and he finds *brahman*
who always sees *brahman*
in all his actions.

4:25   Some seekers
sacrifice
to one god or another.
Others in the fire of *brahman*
sacrifice
the sacrifice itself.

4:26   Some restrain their hearing
in the fire of restraint
and others sacrifice the sound
in the fire of the senses.

4:27   Others offer up the senses

and their vital breath
and burn them in the fire
of self-restraint
that wisdom kindles.

4:28 Some sacrifice material possessions,
practising austerities.
Some do yoga
and others take a vow
to study vedic lore
and sacrifice themselves to knowledge.

4:29 Some control the upward
vital breath
and some the downward
exhalation of the breath.

4:30 Others are restrained in what they eat.
They too control the breath.
All these know the way of sacrifice
and so are freed from sin.

4:31 Those who eat the food
of immortality
remaining from the sacrifice
are reabsorbed in the immortal.
Those who do not sacrifice
get nothing in this world
and have no hope of any other.

4:32 Many kinds of offerings
are laid before the face of *brahman*.
All these are born of action.
Know this and be free.

4:33 The offering of wisdom
is better than material
sacrifices,
for all these
are resolved in wisdom.

*

4:34   Attend humbly to the wise
        who understand the truth.
        Ask and they will teach you,
4:35   then never will you fall
        again into confusion
        but in the light of wisdom see
        all others in yourself,
        yourself in me.

4:36   The greatest sinner even
        may by wisdom
        sail across a sea of wickedness.

4:37   Just as fire
        reduces wood to ashes
        so actions are reduced to ashes
        in the fire of wisdom.

4:38   Nothing can be found
        more purifying than this wisdom.
        He who has perfected it
        in time will find
        that wisdom in the self.

4:39   He who has faith
        attains to wisdom.
        Devoted to it as the highest good,
        subduing all his senses,
        he soon finds supreme peace.

4:40   The ignorant without faith
        - the doubters -
        are lost to this world
        and the next.
        Never will they be at ease.

4:41   Action does not bind one
who abandons it
by following this way,
his doubt cut off by wisdom
and in possession of the self.

4:42   Armed with your sword of wisdom
then, cut off this doubt
that has its roots in ignorance
deep in the heart.
Follow this way!
Stand up!

NOTES ON THE TEXT AND TRANSLATION

Book 4 returns to the way of action (*karma-yoga*) and the nature of the enduring non-acting self that 'does nothing' at all (4:20). The realised self is released from attachment to actions, and implicitly from their karmic fruits or consequences. So released, he is free to make his offerings directly to *brahman*, the highest offering being wisdom (*jnana*) itself. Worship is man's only truly free act. This thought leads on to observations on various forms of sacrifice, contrasting the selfless way of *karma-yoga* with ritual actions and austerities designed to achieve an end that, this teaching asserts, can only be achieved by cutting away this doubtful knowledge with the sword of yogic wisdom.

4:1
changeless way. 'eternal *yoga*'.

Vivasvat, Manu, Ikshvaku. Vivasvat was the sun-god of ancient mythology. Manu was the son of Vivasvat and progenitor of the human race. Ikshvaku was the son of Manu and founder of the mythical royal dynasty descended from the sun. The purpose here is to establish the eternal nature of the teaching by locating it prior to the creation of man.

4:2
the royal line of seers. This verse serves further to establish the lineage of *yoga* as the (secret) doctrine of kings.

4:6
unborn self. The self exists in the eternal present and therefore has no cause in time for coming into being and does not cease to be (see 2:12: 'There never was a time when I was not'). It arises in the material world by its own will in its manifest body in time, over and over again.

THE SONG OF MYSELF

4:7

righteousness. '*dharma*', meaning rightness of duty, in particular the established order of caste duty.

4:9

divine. Krishna is 'divine' in the sense that his realised self has the divine qualities of being 'unborn', eternal and self-manifesting (4:6). And although this verse will sustain a Vaishnavite reading, the consistency of meaning is not lost: by realising the self we free ourselves from the bonds of action – and the bonds of time – and from the cycle of birth and death that arises solely from our continued attachment to the ego and its interests (and we are therefore not reborn). The identification of 'me' with the state of detached self-realisation through the disciplined acquisition of wisdom becomes clear in the next verse (4:10). There is also an element of deliberate antithesis in the verse, balancing the 'coming to me' with the 'departing' of the recyclable body.

4:11

I am their reward. 'thus I reward them'. There is no specific worldly or even heavenly reward denoted by 'thus' other than the reward to be found in following the path to become that same liberated being who speaks as 'me'. It is the nature of this 'reward' that acts as the spur in 4:12 to contrast the two reward systems, the vedic and the yogic. Verses 4:13-23 properly define action and non-action in a wider sense than simply ritual actions, concluding with a restatement of the view that the self's free actions are actions of worship or sacrifice. It is at this point, seemingly triggered by a need to elaborate upon the idea of 'sacrifice', that those doctrinal differences are picked up again in a long passage from 4:24 to 4:33, contrasting the vedic ritual acts of sacrifice with the equivalent but opposite 'offerings' of the *samkhya-yoga* teaching in which the full and final sacrifice is the offering of supreme wisdom.

4:12

instant success. 'Success will surely come quickly' for those who wish for success in the human, material world – in contrast to the harder path of acquiring wisdom.

their gods. The gods of the vedic sacrifices.

4:13

I am. The detached self, the supreme self, identifies itself with the impersonal creative and sustaining principle of the world, including its social order. It does not act itself. That principle, though not named here, is *brahman*.

order in the world. 'the four-caste system' – the inviolable order of society.

determined by the will in nature. 'determined by the interaction of the *gunas*' which are objectively given. The emphasis is on the objective nature of the given order and the objective actions of the *gunas*, created by but not under the direction of their creator, *brahman*.

4:14

Actions. Actions here are actions in the world, in the conduct of life, and do not in this case refer specifically to ritual actions (as they might appear to, given the focus of 4:12). The philosophy of action and non-action is now propounded through to 4:23.

4:15

In ancient times we knew this. 'The ancients having known this' – but 'we' is consistent with the self-identification of Krishna-as-teacher, eternally present through the ages, with the originator of the royal line of ancient wisdom. (See 4:2)

4:16

poets of old. The sages of the past, working in the tradition and composing in verse forms, and therefore probably meaning the authors of the earlier Upanishads.

you will be free. 'you will be released from ills' – the ills arising from attachment to actions.

4:18

non-action in his actions. 'He should perceive non-action in action and action in non-action'. 'Acting without acting' (non-action in action) is the comprehensible message of the teaching, reiterated many times. The reverse of this, seeing action in non-action, is less easy to understand and made more obscure by being phrased for antithesis and euphony: *karmanyakarma yah/akarmani ca karma yah.* But the meaning of the two carefully balanced phrases can be given as: 'Action takes place, yet the self does not act/The self does not act, yet action takes place.' One is non-action (of the self as agent) in action, the other action in non-action (of the non-acting self). Both are conformed to the disciplined wisdom of insight into the true nature of the self and its relation to action.

4:19

Enlightened ones. '*budhas*', 'wise ones'.

wise. 'a *pandit*'. A wise, learned or legally competent man. The *budhas* are 'wise' and the *pandit* is also 'wise'. Apart from providing a variation in the vocabulary in the Sanskrit text, there may be a distinction in wisdom. We are in the early stages of the transition to enlightened understanding of which detachment from the rewards of action is the wise beginning.

the fire of wisdom. The motif of 'fire' will recur in this section both as the fire of wisdom that consumes *karma*, the attachment to actions, and as the sacrificial fire in which, in the vedic rites, offerings are made to the gods, wisdom being the highest of all offerings.

4:20
no dependency on anyone for anything. The Sanskrit text says simply 'not dependent', but it refers back to the freedom from dependency identified in 3:18, which I have glossed here.

4:23
released. Released from the bonds of action. He has made a bonfire of his attachments. As has been consistently indicated, the self's only free action is the act of sacrifice or worship. Nowhere are we far from ritual action in any discussion of action, whether as action on the field of battle or action to sustain the order of the universe. Throughout much of the text there is a heavy anchoring consciousness of the antipathetical doctrinal position of the core teaching in relation to ritually based religious practices, and it is always alert to the need to defend or accommodate that position. We have to remember that no one but kings, princes, *yogins*, *budhas*, *pandits* and Brahmins is listening.

vanish in the act of sacrifice. This is consistent with the earlier statement in 3:9: 'The only action that is free is worship'. In 4:37 that vanishing is developed into the metaphor of a reduction to ashes of actions consumed in the fire of wisdom, wisdom being the ultimate sacrificial offering since it is an offering without attachments, without desires.

4:24
Unsurprisingly, the reintroduction of 'sacrifice' at the

conclusion of the previous verse now opens up the opportunity to say more, in the following sequence of verses, to contrast the selfless 'sacrifice' of the wisdom of the *samkhya-yoga* school of thought with the vedic rites and the austere practices of renunciation and self-control of various other 'seekers'.

For the offering is brahman. The argument up to this point has established that one who is 'firm in wisdom' performs all his actions without attachment to hopes, expectations, desires or preferences, but 'acts without acting' as *brahman* acts without acting in sustaining the order of the world. One's acts of sacrifice, therefore, have no object other than to acknowledge or celebrate that sustaining order. This verse is a description of the motiveless act of sacrifice, placing *brahman* as the one and only legitimate object of the act.

4:25
From here through to 4:33 we have a description of different types of ritual practices or disciplines undertaken by 'adepts' – seekers after wisdom – ranging from ritual sacrifices to the gods to austere practices of self-control. Without some form of active participation in sacrifice nothing is accomplished, not even the possession of this world let alone entry into the next. But they all share the same character: they are actions performed to some end. Only the offering of wisdom has no further end or aim than itself, and in that realisation comes release from the delusion that this singular sort of wisdom can be achieved by such alternative actions as those described.

seekers. '*yogins*', but in this instance the term is not being used solely to mean those firm in the *yoga* discipline but to encompass a variety of 'adepts'.

the fire of brahman. This is the same 'fire' as the fire in 4:24. The fire of *brahman* and the fire of wisdom are both invoked in this verse sequence as the fire in which *karma* is burned up.

4:26

The sacrificial 'fire' metaphor is continued in this verse, which has a certain awkwardness resulting from the insistence on the metaphor and on the antithesis between 'hearing' and 'sound'. The literal reading is: 'Some others offer the senses such as hearing in the fire of restraint. Others offer the objects of the senses such as sounds in the fire of the senses'. The meaning of both sentences is similar: the adept controls his senses or controls what reaches his senses.

4:27

vital breath. 'prana'. A reference to one of the breath control disciplines of *yoga* practice. *Prana* is the in-breath.

the fire of self-restraint. 'the fire of the *yoga* discipline of self-restraint'.

4:28

yoga. I have left *yoga* untranslated here because it is used generically to refer to a heritage of ancient practices not very removed from what is understood by 'yoga' today.

4:29

The two antithetical breath control disciplines of the five yogic energy breathing regimens.

4:31

are reabsorbed in the immortal. 'enter into primal *brahman*'. We have come across this brahmanic reference to the remnant of the sacrifice before in 3:13. Offerings of some sort are necessary just to make the world go round, to turn the wheel (3:16).

4:32

All these are born of action. 'All (sacrifices) originate in action'. Sacrifices are acts not to be avoided by 'non-action'.

free. 'released'. We have variously been offered freedom from delusion, freedom from evil, sin or blame, and freedom from the bonds of action. Here that freedom or release from action (*karma*) and its self-interests is explained again in relation to acts of sacrifice or offerings. Actions, and ritual actions in particular, are necessary and unavoidable. We *should* act – but we have to correctly understand the nature of action and non-action (4:17-18) in order not to be bound to or tainted by (4:14) actions. For one who understands this, his sole work is sacrifice (4:23) – here the implication is that sacrifice in all its forms qualifies – and in this lies his freedom from the bonds of action and from the rituals themselves (3:17).

4:35

all others in yourself, yourself in me. The 'self' here is the shared self of subjective being that all have in common, cognate with the impersonal sustaining power that is *brahman*, in whose behalf the Krishna-teacher speaks again as 'me'.

4:36

'The greatest evil-doer can cross over wickedness by the boat of wisdom.'

4:38

this wisdom/it. 'jnana-yoga'.

4:39

faith. Faith in this doctrine, in contrast to the 'doubters' of 4:40 (those referred to in the doctrinal dispute in 3:31-32).

4:41

this way. 'yoga'.

4:42

deep in the heart. Ignorance is hard to shift, it is so embedded in one's nature, in one's character, bound to it by the interwoven strands of the *gunas*. It is severed with the sword of wisdom, by the *yoga* of wisdom. But Arjuna must *act*, and sever the bonds of doubt arising from ignorance. And, finally, he must *stand up* and fight, for now, at the end of this chapter, we are back at the scene of battle where Arjuna is seated in his chariot.

5

THE LORD OF EVERY GATE

My respiration and inspiration, the beating of my heart,
the passing of blood and air through my lungs
Walt Whitman, *Song of Myself*

5:1   Again you praise
abandonment of actions,
again you praise
the way of action.
Tell me once for all
which of these two ways
is better.

5:2   Abandonment of action
and the way of action
both lead to the highest goal.
But of these two
the way of action
is far better
than renunciation.

5:3   One indifferent
to pain and pleasure,
likes and dislikes,
happily is free
from ties to action –
a constant abstainer.

5:4   The foolish say

that theory and its practice
are different paths.
Learned men say otherwise.
Either followed truly
brings the same reward.

5:5   The two are one.
The followers of both
journey to the same place.

He who sees
sees.

5:6   Renunciation
is not easy to achieve
without a method.
A wise man following
this discipline
will get there
in a little while.

5:7   Harnessed to this discipline
he purifies the self,
subdues the self,
controls his senses
and becomes the self
within the self
of every being.
Actions do not touch him.

5:8   He, holding fast to that,
seeing, hearing, touching,
smelling, eating, walking,
sleeping, breathing,
thinks:
I myself do nothing.

5:9   Speaking,
        grasping or releasing,
        with open eyes
        or closed,
        believes:
        The senses merely live
        among the objects of the senses.

5:10   All his actions
        and attachments
        he abandons
        to the great non-doer.
        Guilt does not mark him,
        no more than water
        on the lotus leaf.

5:11   Those who follow this regime,
        abandoning attachments,
        exercising body, mind
        and understanding,
        or focused only on the senses,
        work to purify the self.

5:12   The disciplined abandoner
        of objects of desire
        finds peace,
        but he without this discipline
        remains in bondage
        to desire.

5:13   Renouncing all
        that rises in the mind
        the self sits happily within
        and rules the city of the senses,
        the lord of every gate.

He neither acts himself
nor causes anything to happen.
5:14   For he is not the agency
of actions in the world
and not their cause,
nor does he connect
an action with the ends of actions
All this flows from nature.

5:15   The self is not affected
by either good or ill
proceeding from the acts
of other people,
whose ignorance conceals
this wisdom
and deludes them.
5:16   But those who have destroyed
their ignorance with wisdom
light up the self
as brightly as the sun.

5:17   Those with minds on that,
centred on that,
founded on that,
holding that to be supreme,
and having cast off guilt
through wisdom,
pass beyond the cycle of rebirth.

5:18   The learned doctors
look upon the wisest Brahmin
and a cow... or elephant...
or dog... or outcaste feeding on a dog
impartially.
5:19   But even here on earth

the cycle of rebirth is overcome
by one whose mind
is equally impartial.
For the sameness
and the guiltlessness of one
abide within the other.

5:20 Not feeling pleased
with what is pleasing
nor displeased
by what displeases,
determined, undeluded,
he knows the eternal,
is stilled in the eternal.

5:21 He who is untouched
by the external
and sufficient in himself,
with effort
touches the eternal
and finds eternal ease.

5:22 The pleasures of the senses
are delivered from the womb of pain
where they begin and end.
The wise find no contentment there.

5:23 He who in this life
bears the agitation of desire
with equanimity,
practising this way,
leads a happy life.

5:24 Such a man
who finds within himself

happiness, contentment
and an inner radiance
comes to know that holy state
of ultimate release
5:25   where ills have passed away
and he has freed himself
from all dualities,
in perfect self-control,
delighting only
in the welfare of all beings.

5:26   For those detached
from love and anger,
those whose thoughts
are under their control,
for those who truly know the self,
this holy state surrounds them.

*

5:27   Subduing all sensation
of the outside world,
focusing attention on
the space between the eyebrows,
equalising inhalation
with the out-breath
through the nostrils,
5:28   in control
of senses, mind and will,
the wise from whom
desire, fear and anger
have departed,
seeking nothing higher
than release
will surely find it.

*

5:29   By sacrifice
he comes to know me,
lord of all the world,
lover of all creatures,
and knowing me
finds peace.

NOTES ON THE TEXT AND TRANSLATION

In response to Arjuna's request for a definitive answer to the better of the two 'ways' or *yogas*, one described as the way of 'renunciation', the other the way of 'action', his master/teacher finally makes a definitive statement in favour of the way of action. However, for anyone who has not fully understood the story so far there is still much room for confusion. For we are told that the two ways are the 'same'. The way that is called 'renunciation' is the way of wisdom of the *samkhya* school that implies in practice an abandonment of the world and its snares. The way of 'action' is the way of exactly the same wisdom, but in abandoning attachment to the world the *yogin* does not abandon action *in* the world (for all the reasons given earlier).

The practice of either requires a discipline (*yoga*) – hence the *yoga* of wisdom (or knowledge), the *yoga* of action and the *yoga* of renunciation given as the usual 'titles' of Books 2, 3 and 5 respectively. That discipline is both a discipline of mental attitude and will and an exercise of control over the body and its faculties to illumine the inner self and free it from attachment to the world of the senses and from actions intended to secure those attachments.

The term *yoga* we now find used with three different shades of meaning. It is used generically to stand for *karma-yoga*, the way of action (or wisdom in action); as a 'method' or technique to achieve the goal of both the way of wisdom (*jnana-yoga*) and the way of action; and thirdly as the goal itself, namely the 'achievement' of *yoga* (we have seen this use earlier in 2:53). This chapter focuses much more on the actual practice of *yoga*, and we come across references to common breath control techniques. The conclusion of the chapter, seemingly wishing to celebrate the 'release' that comes from perfecting that technique, rises up on wings towards Buddhist *nirvana* once more (see 2:72 and Note).

5:3

a constant abstainer. 'he is to be known as an eternal renouncer'. As we have already learned, one who has become indifferent to the 'opposites' of pain and pleasure, desire and hate, likes and aversions, is already free from ties (bondage) to actions (that is, from the aims and ends, from the 'fruits' of action, not from the performance of actions themselves, in which he 'acts without acting'). He is constant in that renunciation in all he does and therefore, implicitly, has no need to renounce the world and its temptations.

5:4

theory and its practice. '*samkhya*' and '*yoga*'.

Learned men. 'The *pandits*'.

brings the same reward. 'he finds the same fruit from both'.

5:5

both. Samkhya is allowed to stand for both the philosophical, rational but disciplined path of understanding and for the 'way of renunciation', the retreat from the world into a contemplative rather than an active discipline of mind. *Yoga* stands for that same understanding retained in action (by the abstaining, non-acting realised self). As we have said before (Notes to 2:50 and 3:3) wisdom in understanding underpins wisdom in action. The two paths lead to the same place – but both require a *method* (*yoga*) to get there.

He who sees sees. The phrasing is deliberately cryptic for poetic effect: *yah pasyati sa pasyati.*

5:6

renunciation – of attachment to the fruits of action.

method/discipline. 'yoga'.

will get there in a little while. 'will reach *brahman* quite quickly'. The goal is now referred to as *brahman*; that is, by renouncing attachment to actions arising from the senses and sense objects we identify the non-acting self with the impersonal sustaining principle, *brahman*. However much the terminology changes (the self, *brahman*, renunciation, highest good, wisdom, *yoga*, supreme peace or, more and more significantly, 'me') the goal is always the same.

5:7
Harnessed to this discipline. Literally, 'Disciplined in discipline', 'Yoked to the yoke' of *yoga*.

Actions do not touch him. 'He is not tainted when acting.'

5:8
holding fast to that. 'yoked to *yoga*'.

5:9
the senses. Unattached to the idea of the ego and its objects, he accepts all sensations indifferently because 'they are not mine' but belong to the realm of the senses and their sensed objects.

5:10
to the great non-doer. 'to *brahman*', the indifferent sustainer of the world who does nothing. The devolution of action to *brahman* was first counselled in 3:30.

5:11
Those who follow this regime. 'yogins'.

or focused only on the senses. Meaning, to practise keeping the senses in check.

5:13

Renouncing all that rises in the mind. The usual interpretation of this line is, 'Renouncing all actions "with" or "by" the mind'. The alternative is 'in' the mind, which I believe is what is meant in this context. *Manas*, the mind, is a passive instrument. If the verse were again referring to the mind's 'control' of the senses then *buddhi* would be expected here. The image conjured up is certainly that of a *yogin* seated in a mindful state, in charge of his senses and the prompts to action that arise in the mind to distract the pure embodied self within (*dehi*).

the city of the senses. 'the city with nine gates' – the body and its nine orifices through which the external world enters and departs.

5:17

that. The supreme self.

5:18

learned doctors. '*pandits*'.

impartially, because they are all various conditions of birth, of the perishable forms of coming into and going out of being in the endless cycle of rebirth. Under the eye of eternity they are all the same.

5:19

For the sameness and the guiltlessness of one abide within the other. 'For they abide within (partake of) the guiltlessness and impartiality of *brahman*.' 5:18 and 5:19 should be read in conjunction. In 5:18 we are told about the orthodox beliefs of the Brahmins and *pandits* who are learned in the knowledge and lore of the Vedas and the rituals relating to rebirth and the passage from life to death. The elephant may, of course, have once been a man. Rebirth is something to be avoided. (It is fruitless to investigate too far into the theory of rebirth to determine who or what gets reborn as an elephant.) Viewing these all impartially, seeing them as the same, leads in 5:19 to the idea that endless rebirths before one reaches a perfected state can be avoided, and perfection achieved in one lifetime. That conquest of rebirth (the same thing over and over again with nothing to illuminate, and thereby end, the endless passage to and fro in darkness) lies in becoming equally impartial (to the opposites). *Brahman* is the impartial sustainer of the world but does not act (and therefore, lacking intentionality, incurs no guilt). The self (*atman*) is the same, neither agent nor cause, free from actions (*karma*) and the ends of actions, free from 'blame', free, as we shall see, from the 'perishable' forms of life. Seeing things as the same, and being the same, one is established in the other, *atman* in *brahman*, and therefore, in realising this, one escapes the cycle of rebirth which, we should recall, is brought about solely by desire, by differentiating good from bad, by preferences, loves and hates, by clinging to the self-interests of our actions. This teaching is recognisably the Buddhist path of negation and emancipation from the wheel of birth and death.

5:20
determined. 'firm in discriminating intellect (*buddhi*)'.

eternal. '*brahman*'.

5:21
effort. '*yoga*'.

touches. 'is united with'. The antithetical phrasing in the original text balances 'unattached' (translated as 'untouched') with 'united with' or, literally, 'yoked to' (touches).

is…sufficient in himself/finds…ease. 'finds happiness'/'reaches happiness'. The Sanskrit in each case is *sukha*, 'happiness', a recurring word in the *Gita* that has to stand for a number of happy emotional conditions, from the rather bland 'pleasantness' to the more extremes of 'joy' and 'bliss'. These latter seem inappropriate in the context of inner tranquillity and ease 'fixed in the eternal', or of freedom from pain as described in the following verses. The description is of a settled condition rather than an excitable state of mind. See also Note to 6:28.

5:22
That all life is suffering, and all pleasures have an end, is the essential realisation at the heart of Buddhist doctrine.

5:23
in this life. 'before he is released from the body'.

this way. 'yoga'.

leads a happy life. 'is a happy man', 'is a man at ease'.

5:24
Such a man. 'The *yogin*'.

comes to know that holy state of ultimate release. Literally, 'is absorbed into *brahman* and extinguished in *brahma-nirvana*', in the impersonal thing-in-itself that is *brahman*. To now identify this unification of *brahman-atman* with *brahma-nirvana*, with the falling away of the self and all its attributes, with the complete negation of the self, would seem at this point a step too far that does not follow reasonably from what has preceded it. There is doubtless an effort here to equate the Buddhist state of enlightened selflessness with the realisation of the self in *brahman*, but the effort has not included the unravelling of the illusion of the self that in Buddhist disciplined practice is the *sine qua non* of ultimate release.

5:25
Dualities have not been mentioned before (though 'opposites' have). This is pure Buddhist doctrine locating *nirvana* in the state of release from suffering and the illusion of dualities, with the enlightened self working solely for the welfare of the world.

5:29
By sacrifice. 'As the object of the sacrifice of austerities'. See 4:24-4:33.

6

THE CONQUERED SELF

In all people I see myself Walt Whitman, *Song of Myself*

6:1   He who acts
       without self-interest
       but does what must be done
       is a renouncer,
       a follower of the way,
       not he who does without the fire
       and the sacrifice.

6:2   Renunciation
       is the essence of this way.
       There is no way
       without renunciation
       of self-interest.

6:3   The wise man
       who desires to find the way
       pursues the way of action.
       He who has already found it
       holds quietly to it.

6:4   When not attached
       to objects of the senses
       or to the objects
       of his actions,
       and purposeless,
       then it can be said
       that he has found the way.

6:5   The self should raise
the self
and not let down
the self.
For only the self
is a friend to the self,
and only the self
is its enemy.

6:6   For one who has conquered
the self is a friend
but the unconquered self
is a threat,
like an enemy.

6:7   The conquered self
is at peace with the self
through heat and cold,
in pain and pleasure,
honour and disgrace.

6:8   The self-sufficient self
contents itself
with knowledge of the self.
He has reached
fulfilment of this discipline
who stands above the fray,
a conqueror of the senses,
to whom a stone,
a clod of earth, or gold
are all the same.

6:9   He who sees the same
in friend or enemy,
companion and kinsman,
who equally regards
the righteous and unrighteous,

is the supreme man.

*

6:10   Concentrating
only on the self,
he sits
secluded and alone,
his thoughts subdued,
desiring nothing,
possessing nothing.

6:11   He firmly sits
in some place clean and pure,
covered first with fragrant grass,
a deerskin, then a cloth,
placed neither high nor low.

6:12   Focused on a single point,
subduing thoughts and senses,
he sits
and practices this discipline
to purify the self.

6:13   With body, head and neck erect,
motionless he sits,
focused on the point of his nose
and looking nowhere else.

6:14   With quietude of mind
and all fears put away
he dedicates himself to abstinence.
His thoughts controlled,
he sits and concentrates
on me alone, the higher self.

6:15   And so by constancy
and diligence in practice
he finally subdues the mind
and finds tranquillity and peace
absorbed in me.

6:16   But know:
       this way is not the way
       for those who eat too much
       nor those who fast,
       for those who sleep too much
       nor those who keep themselves awake.
6:17   In all things,
       eating, sleeping,
       work and play,
       moderation is the way
       that ends unhappiness.

6:18   He is known
       for firmness of the mind
       who once abides
       within the self alone,
       with thoughts subdued,
       free from lust and longing.
6:19   Like a lantern
       in a windless place,
       unwavering
       (the simile comes to mind)
       is one who practises
       self-discipline.
6:20   When the mind
       is stilled by practice
       the self sees in the self
       its own sufficiency.
6:21   Endless happiness is his
       who knows the truth
       beyond the senses
       and abides in it
       and never moves from it.
6:22   Once having found it
       he can think of nothing higher

and the deepest sorrow even
will not move him.

6:23 Let this be the end of pain,
let this be the way,
practised with determination
and an unswayed mind.

6:24 Utterly abandoning
desires arising
from self-interest,
subduing in the mind
the welling up
of all the senses

6:25 by his will,
he should slowly
come to rest
within the self,
letting go
all other thoughts,

6:26 and when
the wandering mind
begins to wander
bring it back
within the self.

6:27 For one whose mind
finds peace
in which all passions cease
and evils vanish
the self is one
with the eternal,
the highest realm of bliss.

6:28 Through constant practice
in this way,
readily
he comes to be at one
with the eternal,

all ills banished,
finding everlasting bliss.

*

6:29   He sees the self
in every being,
all beings in the self.
He knows them as the same.

6:30   He sees me
in all things,
all things
he sees in me.
I am not lost to him
nor he to me.

6:31   Who comes to me
abides in me
as one.
In all his acts
he acts in me.

6:32   To him
all things,
the good, the bad,
are one in him.

6:33   But how can one sustain
this evenness of mind?
It wanders as it wills.

6:34   The mind is wilful,
as powerful and stormy
as the wind and just
as hard to tame.

6:35   Indeed the restless mind
        resists control,
        but yet by practice
        and indifference to the world
        it may be tamed.

6:36   I think the final goal
        is hard to reach
        by one unable to control
        the self,
        but possible
        with proper effort.

6:37   What happens to the one
        who, though believing,
        fails to master his own
        mind and self?

6:38   Is he not lost
        to this world and the next,
        drifting like a cloud,
        deluded,
        with no solid path to follow?

6:39   Help me to erase this doubt
        for no one else can help me.

6:40   He who has faith
        is never lost to virtue

6:41   but dwells
        where merit dwells
        for endless years
        then comes again
        to dwell among the good
        and well-born,

6:42   or even finds himself

reborn among the wise,
though this is harder to achieve,
6:43 picking up again the thread
of former knowledge,
ever striving onwards.
6:44 His former practice
has its own momentum.
Even just the wish
to know this path
takes him farther
than mere ritual chanting.
6:45 By perseverance and restraint
he purifies himself of evils,
perfects himself through many births
until at last he finds
the supreme goal.

6:46 The follower of this discipline
is more than an ascetic,
greater than a learned man
who knows the rites
and higher than the man
performing them.
Become this man!

6:47 Of these the one
surrendering his inmost self to me
and who with faith devotes himself to me
is said to have the greatest discipline of all.

NOTES ON THE TEXT AND TRANSLATION

Book 6 continues the theme of renunciation and detachment, indifference and equanimity of mind. We have learned briefly in the previous chapter something of the breath-control techniques of *yoga*. In this book, beginning at 6:10, we have a short treatise on the techniques of concentration and meditation which continues through to 6:28 and the apotheosis of the self absorbed in *brahman*. Then, at 6:37, Arjuna raises another doubt. What becomes of the man who makes the attempt to follow the way of *yoga* and its discipline, but fails to achieve that final goal? The answer comes as a reassurance that no effort is entirely lost. The *yogin* is reborn and, by cumulative increments over many lifetimes, realises the self. Arjuna is urged, finally, to become this man, a *yogin*. The very last verse personifies the voice of the united state of *brahman-atman*, anticipating the change of tone and direction in the *Gita* that begins with Book 7.

6:1

a follower of the way. 'a *yogin*'. It is self-interest that is being renounced, not action itself, not the actions that are one's duty. Read more narrowly in relation to ritual actions, the *yogin* must renounce the expected fruits of the rites and not simply abandon their performance (the fire and the sacrifice), reasserting at this point the primacy of the rites from which, as we learned earlier (3:17), the *yogin* is free.

6:2

There is no way. 'No one becomes a *yogin*'.

6:3

to find the way. 'to ascend to *yoga*'. Here '*yoga*' is used in the sense of a goal to be reached.

pursues the way of action. 'action is the method'. There are two 'ways', as iterated in 3:3, each requiring a 'method': the action-without-attachment method of *karma-yoga* practice, or the quietist method of *jnana-yoga*. For one, action is the method, for the other quiescence is the method. One works towards, the other rests within.

6:4
he has found the way. 'he has ascended to *yoga*'.

6:5

> *And that unlesse above himselfe he can*
> *Erect himselfe, how poore a thing is man?*[1]

Clearly we have two selves here. One is the lower-case self and the other the upper-case Self, the 'supreme self' (*atman* is employed for both). The 'self' can be interpreted as the 'will'. It can either make the effort to rise to the supreme self by conquering the self-will of the ego and its attachments, or it can succumb to the forces of the will (the *gunas* at work in the self), the enemy of the higher Self, the self as one's own worst enemy. The concision of this passage and the use of antithesis ('to raise'/'to let down', 'self'/'self', 'friend'/'enemy') turns it into a riddle.

6:8
knowledge of the self. '*jnana-vijnana*' – the realisation of wisdom. *Jnana* (knowledge) is 'wisdom'. *Vijnana* is 'strong knowledge' or 'realisation'. It is one thing to acquire knowledge, another to be wise, but something else to have realised what you know and what you have learned through thinking and practice and made it your own at the centre of your being. When this chapter ends we move on to the

---

[1] Daniel, Samuel. *To the Lady Margaret, Countess of Cumberland* (1603).

celebration of that realisation of the self in experience.

6:9
the supreme man. 'he is distinguished (or superior) among men', but in English the choice of either word would invite a contradiction of the even-mindedness prescribed. The 'supreme man' is the *yogin.*

This verse seems to take us back to the field of battle in a conclusive way, neatly ending this section which is abruptly followed by a digression on the practice of meditation.

6:18
He is known for firmness of the mind. 'He is known as disciplined'.

6:19
the simile comes to mind. We appear here to catch a mind in the spontaneous act of creation in a work whose authorship is otherwise obscure.

practises self-discipline. 'disciplined in performing the *yoga* of the self'.

6:23
let this be the way. 'let this be called *yoga*'.

unswayed. 'undismayed', 'undespairing', referring to the end of sorrow and pain above.

6:27
the eternal. 'brahman'.

6:28
this way. 'yoga'.

readily. 'easily', 'happily'. (Compare with 4:39 where he 'soon', or 'quickly', attains peace.)

all ills banished. 'Ills' and its cognates (evils, wrongs, stains, blame) have been used constantly in the text. The 'ills' are the ills of earthly existence arising from attachment to the senses, to desires, hopes and ambitions, and to the 'fruits' of action that has been the central theme of these first books of the *Gita.* Hovering nearby is the more difficult question of 'guilt' and the freedom of the *yogin* from personal responsibility for the 'evils' that may arise from his own (selfless) actions. See my concluding essay, *Action, non-action and devotion.*

bliss. '*sukha*'. There are various gradients of 'happiness' attached to '*sukha*', including pleasantness at one degree, rising to 'joy' and 'bliss' in the right context. The underlying meaning is 'ease', and the root word is used with this meaning earlier in the verse where it speaks of 'readily' or 'easily' reaching *brahman.* Given that the *yogin* ideally sees happiness and unhappiness as the same (the obverse of *sukha* is *duhkha*) his ideal should properly be interpreted not as supreme 'happiness' but perfect 'ease'. To be at ease in the world is to accept happiness and pain alike, at ease with either, 'a season of our inner year', as Rilke says.[1] Although I have gone along for the most part with a conventional translation of '*sukha*' we should avoid confusing the ease that comes with the peace of understanding with anything resembling impassioned mystical ecstasy. (See also Note to 5:21.) Verse 6:28 is essentially a reiteration of 6:27.

6:29
He. 'He who is disciplined in *yoga*'.

---

[1] Rilke, Rainer Maria. *The Tenth Elegy* in *Duino Elegies* (1923).

6:29/6:30
See the parallel statement in 4:35

6:31
he acts in me. See the parallel opening line of 3:30

6:32
the good, the bad. 'ease and dis-ease'.

6:40-6:45
Though irrational, there is something compellingly reasonable in the understandable aversion to the idea that virtue in this world should find no fulfilment but merely expire with the last breath, that the good is just as lost to oblivion as evil is when death intrudes to bring its reign to an end. The belief in natural justice, that good should be rewarded and evil punished, is the psychological foundation of both heaven and hell. What in this world has clearly been observed as injustice will be put right in the next.

Sociologically and culturally, to believe that virtue is really wasted is a dangerous belief. We have discovered so far, in references to the orthodox doctrine of rebirth running through the *Gita*, that those who are driven by their passions, by self-interest, worldly rewards and attachment to the aims and ends of their actions are reborn and condemned to repeat their lives. The evidence, should we need any, is observable all around us (and in ourselves). But the *yogin* can free himself in this lifetime, in this world, and has no need of ritual actions, sacrifices, rites and chanting for the purposes of increasing his chances of a better life in a new incarnation. The *yogin* performs ritual actions solely because they are meritorious in their own right; they are selfless acts of worship or devotion. The question now is, what about the man who takes up this path and pursues it to the best of his endeavour, but fails to achieve the final goal of self-realisation, whose will fails him, whose mind remains confused? Is all his effort lost, drifting away like mist across a path that is too hard to follow? So we have the idea that virtue is cumulative, that we can get there little by little over many lifetimes (more quickly if we are reborn into a family already versed in yogic wisdom). And no doubt we should not deter the virtuous from virtue or from believing in the incremental benefit to the whole world over time of behaving virtuously oneself, or dismiss the effort on no safer ground than the absence of any definable entity or soul that migrates from one life to another. In any case, in this philosophy virtue is its own reward, for when we act the self does not act, it has no end or aim or attachment or reward in mind, only duty or doing what must be done. In this way nothing is ever lost, for nothing was intended, nothing was to be gained.

6:44

ritual chanting. Vedic recitation. The contrast is again drawn between the path of *yoga* and vedic ritual practices. The same point has been made in 2:40: 'A little effort, even, is not lost.'

6:46

The follower of this discipline. 'The *yogin*'. This verse is a final assertion of the superiority of *yoga* to other contemporary doctrines and ascetic practices, in particular to the emptiness of the vedic rites for one who knows the higher path of *yoga*.

6:47

Of these. Of the *yogins* who practise this way. Their highest achievement is not only to have arrived at an equanimity of mind and detachment from the motivations of action, but to have realised the self in the impersonal and eternal sustaining power of the world, in *brahman-atman* (or *brahma-nirvana*). From this perspective there can be nothing higher, nothing more fulfilling, nothing of greater value, nothing in fact more absolute. From this point on in the *Gita* we hear that absolute voice of the persona of the merged self that speaks at once for the whole cosmos and for the whole of subjective consciousness, who wears the world like a necklace of pearls and to whom, in our new-found freedom, we are, and must be, and cannot help but be devoted. It is likely, however, that this equivocal verse, right at the end of the chapter, was inserted to create a link to a 'devotional' (*bhakti*) reading of the next chapter, for it could also be translated as: 'Of these, the one who comes to me with all his heart and worships me in faith is my greatest devotee.'

7

I AM THE FRAGRANCE OF THE EARTH

I am an acme of things accomplish'd, and I an encloser of things to be.
Walt Whitman, *The Song of Myself*

7:1   Listen! Have no doubt
that he who practises this way,
his mind intent on me,
who finds in me his refuge,
shall surely know me.

7:2   To you I shall explain completely
both this knowledge
and its realisation.
Once understood,
then there is nothing more
on earth to know.

7:3   Of thousands
scarcely one
strives for perfection,
and scarcely one
of those who strive
and even one of those
who reach perfection
really knows me.

7:4   My elemental nature
has eight parts:
earth and air
and fire and water,

the aether, mind,
the will, that self
that manifests itself
as 'I'.

7:5   That is my lower nature.
But know I have a higher nature,
a higher life
by which the whole world
is sustained.

7:6   Understand,
all beings
are descended
from my higher nature.
The world arises
and dissolves
in me.

7:7   For there is nothing higher.
I wear the universe itself
like pearls strung on a thread.

7:8   I am the taste
of the waters.
I am the radiance
of the sun and moon.
I am the sacred syllable
OM
and the sound of it
on the air,
and I am the manhood of men.

7:9   I am the fragrance
of the earth
and the brilliance of fire.

I am the life
in every being,
I am austerity
in the austere,
7:10   the primal seed
of every being,
the intellect
in the intelligent,
the glory of the glorious
7:11   and the might of the mighty
who are free
from passion and desire,
and I am that desire
in beings that accords with duty.

7:12   All three states of being
come from me.
They are in me
but I am not in them.
7:13   The whole world
is deluded by them
and therefore does not know me,
I who am above them
and eternal,
7:14   for they were made in heaven
and are hard to overcome.
Only those who come to me
for refuge see through this illusion.

7:15   The lowest and most evil men
never see me, for illusion
has deprived them of all wisdom
and they live like demons.

7:16   Good men honour me:

those who suffer,
those who seek
power from knowledge,
those who would find wealth,
and the one who knows.

7:17   Of these the noblest
is the one who knows,
steadfast in his wisdom
and devoted
to this one thing only.
And he is dear to me
and I am dear to him.

7:18   All are noble,
but the man who knows
is said to be
myself,
steadfastly abiding in
myself,
the final goal.

7:19   The wise man
after many births
will come to me
and think:
This is all.
Such great souls are rare.

7:20   Men whose wisdom
has been swept away
by this or that desire
seek out other gods
and practise this or that
religious rite.
It is their nature.

7:21   Wherever faith is found
and in whatever form it takes,
I grant it.

7:22   And where the wishes
of the faithful are fulfilled
by these propitiations,
it is I who grant them.

7:23   But such rewards are fleeting
for those of little understanding.
Let those who want them have their gods,
but let the one who loves me come to me.

7:24   The ignorant think
that I am manifest among them,
for they do not know
my higher being,
eternal and transcendent.

7:25   I do not manifest myself
to them
for I am hidden
in illusion.
They do not see me
as I am,
unborn and undying.

7:26   O Arjuna, I know
the living and the dead
and all those yet to be,
but no one,
no one in the world
knows me!

7:27   All men are deluded
       from their birth
       by hatred and desire,
       by all the opposites
       and their deluding power
       arising in them.

7:28   But those who have succeeded
       in bringing to an end that evil,
       pure in deeds and freed
       from the delusion of those opposites,
       pledge themselves to me.

7:29   They seek their refuge here in me
       who strive towards release
       from birth and death.
       And they will know these things completely:
       the universe in all its power,
       the supreme self,
       and action.

7:30   Those who know me
       as the supreme spirit
       and as God,
       who know me as the highest sacrifice,
       even at the hour of death
       they know me
       and are not perturbed.

NOTES ON THE TEXT AND TRANSLATION

With Book 7 we enter a new phase. So far, Arjuna, the listener, has been introduced by Krishna, the teacher, to the *yogas* of knowledge and action, the disciplined path towards detachment from desire and the ends of action and the recognition of the unity of the unconditioned self (*atman*) with the non-acting but sustaining principle of the universe (*brahman*). Krishna now undertakes (7:2) to explain both that knowledge (*jnana*) and its realisation (*vijnana*) in the full understanding of the self. He takes on more fully the persona of the *brahman-atman* and speaks with a voice emanating from that realised state to which the *yogin* is to aspire. He is both the undeluded self that realises its true nature and the impersonal and unmanifest sustainer of the world who 'wears the universe itself like pearls strung on a thread' (7:7).

He is also the source of the will in nature, the *gunas* that give rise to the passions, desires and temperaments of men. One aspect of man's natural inclinations is to seek out gods and find rewards and compensations for his earthly existence and his suffering in this world. But while there is something noble in that tendency, the fruits of worship are only temporary – they are not the way to achieve release from the wheel of birth and death. There is only one true sacrifice, as we have learned before (5:29), and that is the offering of the wisdom of the self, and, as we learn in this chapter, to be devoted to 'me', to find refuge in 'me', to 'know me', hard though it is for men to achieve because their understanding is led astray by the *gunas*, those naturally tendencies to see only the illusory world of appearances and nothing higher. In 7:23 we are told, in a memorable line, that those who worship the gods 'go to the gods'. They are blind to the possibility of their own self-realisation.

We can hardly read the latter part of this chapter without being reminded of the Old Testament command:

'Thou shalt have no other gods before me'. Krishna, here, is not God. It is true that the self, like our conception of God, is omnipresent ('The world arises and dissolves in me') and omniscient ('I know the living and the dead and all those yet to be'). But it is the self, not God, that is 'all'(7:19), 'eternal and transcendent' (7:24). We should not rush to translate this psychological position, this state of mind (for it is nothing else but a state of mindful realisation) into an externally revealed entity in the universe that is all-present and all-knowing but is *not* the self. To introduce God, as agent and creator, would be to undermine the very foundation and aim of this teaching, captured succinctly in 7:29: the complete understanding of 'the universe in all its power, the supreme self, and action'. We learn here that there is nothing higher than the self. If the self is the highest then even God cannot be higher, and if we insist on Him as the equivalence of the highest, as we may, then we must learn to recognise Him subsisting in the act of devotion itself (see 3:15 for an early expression of this).

7:1
his refuge. See 4:8 *et seq.* for a parallel.

7:2
knowledge. 'jnana' – knowledge or wisdom.

realisation. 'vijnana'.

7:3
really knows me. It is clear from this verse, and from the similar plea in 7:26, that, then as now, those few who follow the way and even succeed in it, in terms of abandoning attachment and achieving a state of inner contentment, nonetheless still fail to grasp the real nature of the integrated self.

7:4

elemental nature. '*prakriti*', material nature.

will. '*buddhi*'.

that self. The ego, the faculty of self-consciousness that gives rise to the sense of the ego-self, the 'I' that acts and seeks its reward of happiness in this world.

These eight elements are the standard components of man's material nature in the *samkhya* schemata. Note that mind, the will (*buddhi*) and the self-as-ego are considered to be elements of our material nature; that is, they are materially orientated functions of matter, of the instinctive self-interests of the organism, and linked directly with the functions of the sense organs. Though we might consider the mind, with its will and the sense of self, to be more 'abstract' than this, the essential nature of the mind is functional and practical. Like the heart, it is an instrument to serve the body, and as such, therefore, material and not 'spiritual'.

7:5

a higher life. '*jiva-bhuta*', the vital 'spirit' of the universe from which, in the *samkhya* system, material nature is descended. That is to say, there is always in this philosophy (as in many others and, one way or another, in every religion) an undefinable and unmanifest 'other', an intelligent but, in this case, non-acting originator of 'nature' and nature's material manifestation. This 'spirit' is equated with the non-acting self freed from ignorance and delusion, from the self that thinks it acts but actually always acts from the motivations of its material nature (the *gunas*) and its (material) mind's attachment to the world of its interests and desires. That higher life, that higher self, is the realised self that knows (and in that knowledge wears the universe like a necklace of pearls) and, in this teaching, is the self that is to be known when Krishna says 'know me'.

7:7
This is a pivotal verse in the *Gita* that introduces a more unapologetic, assertive and declamatory style of exposition. Once the 'me' of the higher, supreme self has come out, as it were, as the highest form of being to which, as pure consciousness of being, the entire universe is subject and by which everything that exists is suspended like a necklace of pearls, then the self is released from the constraints of self-explanation to take up any poetic metaphor available to it to express its all-pervading persona as the great 'I am'.

7:8
OM, now quite commonly written *'AUM'* in order to distinguish its three component sounds, is the sacred syllable of *brahman,* the wordless, non-discursive affirmation of the imperishable vital principle of the world. It begins and ends vedic ritual recitation.

7:9
in the austere. 'in those who practise austerity', the ascetics.

7:10
intellect. '*buddhi*', the intelligence or discriminating judgment.

7:11
duty. '*dharma*'. Here we return to the theme of action without agency (the agents of action, the *gunas*, come up in the next verse) and the 'duty' that justifies action, taking us back for a moment to the original argument at the scene of the battle.

7:12
All three states of being. 'The (given) states of being which are

sattvic, rajasic and *tamasic*. The *gunas* are the three 'strands' of a man's temperament and character, his behaviour and disposition. They are not found alone but always woven together in varying proportions. *Rajas* is the active element and is generally understood to be the source of the passions and the initiator of actions arising from attachment. *Tamas* is the 'dark' element and the contrary of *rajas* – not 'unattached', but unmotivated, neglectful, lazy, subversive, deluded. ('Irresolution, sloth, fickleness, despondency, pusillanimity... You surrender your liver to the dark vulture of gloom, and with a frantic stupidity spend your time eating out your heart.'[1]) *Sattva* is the 'light' element, the 'good', the balanced, the realistic, the reasonable. They are each in their own way forms of attachment that bind the self to its material nature and its naturally deluded mind, and a shift towards the dominance of the *sattvic* in a temperament should not be mistaken for a step towards liberation. We are as much attached to our good deeds as we are to our selfish acts and to the temptations of indolence and inaction.

The *gunas* are part of the *samkhya* descriptive system of the 'constituents' of material nature. They will not, of course, stand too much scientific scrutiny. They are descriptive rather than analytical. They are pragmatic representations of the uncontrolled will in nature. The *gunas* are given in nature. They are not within the control of our willing; they are willed already and we have to deal with them. To that extent we cannot look for their agency in the self. They act, they motivate action, but no one sets them in motion. This is why the 'self' declares that the *gunas* are 'in me' as their non-acting originator and that the self is not 'in them' as agent, as the one who acts.

---

[1] Amiel, Henri Frédéric. *The Private Journal of Henri Frédéric Amiel*, translated by Van Wyck Brooks and Charles Van Wyck Brooks. New York: Macmillan, 1935. (Journal entry for May 23, 1855).

7:14

made in heaven. 'divine the *guna*-constructed power of illusion', in the sense that the *gunas* are part of creation but delude the 'whole world' by binding the self to its material nature and blinding it to the imperishable true self.

7:16

Good men. Those who are not completely blinded by illusion and locked into their evil ways like 'the lowest and most evil men'.

those. 'There are four kinds of good men who honour me'. Those who turn away from evil towards God or the gods do so from one of four motives common to all religions and, here, more specifically in relation to the ritual actions and 'sacrifices' of the vedic religion: comfort and release from suffering; (magical) power through knowledge; wealth and good fortune (through possession of that knowledge); the desire for wisdom. This latter motive is the noblest one.

7:17

he is dear to me. The one who holds the highest conception of the self is also the one most esteemed by the self.

7:19

This is all. 'Krishna (identified with *brahman*) is all.'

such great souls. 'such a great self (*mahatma*)'.

7:22

it is I who grant them. – as the originator of the material nature of men and their desires and of the 'wheel' that turns (see 3:15-3:16).

7:23

Let those who want them have their gods. 'Those who worship the gods go to the gods'. 'Those' are the same ones mentioned above who, their minds clouded by illusion, seek only the fulfilment of their material desires, binding them to their actions and to the wheel of birth and death. See also 9:23-9:25 for a development of the text in 7:21-7:23.

7:29

the universe in all its power. 'brahman'.

the supreme self. 'adhyatman'.

action. 'karma'. Brahman, adhyatman and *karma* are the three consolidated themes of this teaching, the self integrated with *brahman* which acts without acting.

7:30

This verse concludes the contrast that has been developed between the ritual worship of the gods ('those who worship the gods go to the gods') and those who truly understand and come to the supreme self ('the one who loves me comes to me'), crowning the development of all that has gone before by raising the condition of *brahman-atman* to equivalence with God. If this is the highest condition we can come to, valid even at the hour of death, then there can be nothing higher, and if we are devoted to the highest and unwavering in that devotion, then we are men of supreme faith, and what else, we should ask ourselves, can be the object of the absolute of faith but what we know as God? Faith, not God, redeems man.

For an explanation of the terms in this verse, see the introductory Note to Book 8 and the Notes to 8:1 and 8:2.

8

THE ETERNAL POET

*(No array of terms can say how much I am at peace about God and
about death.)* Walt Whitman, *Song of Myself*

8:1   Tell me what is meant
by all these terms:
the universe in all its power,
the supreme self
and action,
and the supreme spirit.
And what is God?

8:2   What also is the highest sacrifice,
in this body here and now,
and how do men
who practise self-control
come to know you
at the hour of death?

8:3   The supreme power
is that which is eternal.
The supreme self
is common to all beings
and gives rise to them.
Action is creative cause.

8:4   The supreme spirit
is nature in the transient
forms of being,
and what is meant by God
is divine agency.

The highest sacrifice is me,
the self embodied here and now.

8:5   He who recollects me
at the hour of death
assumes my disembodied
state of being.
Have no doubt of this.

8:6   Whatever state of being
he is mindful of
when he surrenders at the end
his mortal frame,
then that is what
he will become.

8:7   So think of me,
remember me,
and fight!
Trust your mind and will to me
and you will surely come to me.

8:8   He whose mind is disciplined
and not distracted,
thinking only of this one
divine and supreme spirit,
shall arrive at it.

8:9   Think of me as the eternal poet and ruler,
smaller than the smallest thing,
by whom all things are formed,
and yet whose own form is unthinkable,
the colour of the sun, beyond all darkness.

8:10   Who thinks thus
at the final hour,
devoted and with mind unmoved

in strength of discipline,
focusing the vital breath
and his attention
on the centre of his brow,
will come to this
divine and supreme spirit.

8:11 Let me tell you briefly now
about the path that these men follow,
the ones versed in the Vedas
and the passionless ascetics
who have taken vows of chastity
to reach that state to which
they give the name of the eternal.

8:12 He shuts the nine gates
of the body and shuts up
the mind within the heart,
focusing in yogic concentration
on the head and vital breath,

8:13 pronouncing *OM*,
renouncing his own body,
recollecting only me
and setting forth
towards the supreme goal.

8:14 He finds me easily
who thinks of me
with constancy
and never wavers.

8:15 Those great souls
who have through me
attained perfection
do not go to be reborn
into this fugitive world of tears.

8:16 As far as the creator's realm
worlds are born and born again

but he who reaches me
does not return.

8:17   Those who know
the endless day
and endless night
of Brahma
know day and night.

8:18   Out of the unmanifest
comes the manifest,
the visible day,
dissolving again
into invisible night.

8:19   Multitudes of beings
born and reborn in the world
perish, helpless, with
the coming of the night,
returning after many ages
when the day returns.

8:20   But there is something else,
unmanifest,
not that primeval state
of the unmanifest
but something higher,
not lost when all these beings perish.

8:21   This is the eternal
and imperishable supreme goal,
my highest dwelling place,
from which there is no
setting forth again.

8:22   This is the highest state of being,
reached only through devotion to it.
It lies within all beings
and spins out all the universe.

*

8:23   But now I'll speak
about the time
at which a *yogin*
will return or not return
when he departs at death.

8:24   The one who knows
goes to the eternal
in the fire, in the light,
in the brightness of the moon,
in the ascendant sun.

8:25   But he is born again
who leaves by moonlight,
who departs in smoke,
in darkness,
in the descendant
course of the sun.

8:26   These are the two ways
of the universe
through all eternity,
one light, one dark.
By one he goes
and never comes again,
but by the other he returns.

8:27   Knowing that there are
two paths
the *yogin* is not led astray.
Be dedicated to the one path always!

8:28   Having learned from this,
he takes up his original
and highest state of being
beyond the merit to be gained
from vedic lore and sacrifices,
austerities and gifts.

NOTES ON THE TEXT AND TRANSLATION

Book 7 concludes by integrating *adhibhuta* (the realm of the supreme person or spirit), *adhidaivata* (the domain of God) and *adhiyajna* (the ground of the sacrifice) with the 'all' that is the 'me' of this poem. All three terms are, strictly speaking, aspects of being rather than things in themselves, and certainly not separate beings.

Now Arjuna calls for a further explanation of these 'terms' – for we are now straying into the enumerative hierarchy of being of the *samkhya* that will lead us, almost inevitably, to a further description of the theory of rebirth and the active realms of matter and spirit, where it is easy to lose track of the three consolidated themes of 7:29 in the tangle of their mythological roots.

The definition of those terms, briefly given and explained no further, locates *brahman*, as we have already come to know it, as the 'imperishable and eternal' sustainer of creation. *Adhyatma* is the 'highest self'. In this philosophy it is the originator of beings in their material and perishable forms. In theory, if the supreme self is the highest condition of being to which we can ascend, conversely any lower level of material or attached or embodied existence must descend from that higher state. In other words, the 'I am', the *'sum'* of Descartes, can, should and must precede and then outlast its perishable incarnation. *Karma* is action as agency, the creative, from which everything arises, the cause of all subsequent events. *Adhibhuta* we might gloss as 'nature in action', giving rise to the perishable forms of being. *Adhidaivata* is 'divine agency', at work in the rites and sacrifices, to which the supreme self as the 'highest sacrifice' (*adhiyajna*) or object of faith is superior, and through whom all those divine actions are granted. We may therefore understand the meaning of 7:30 in its entirety to be: 'Those who know me, know me to contain within my highest self the origin of every being in nature and of all divine actions, and that I am the supreme object of faith, a faith in which they are unwavering even at the hour of death.'

But we have yet another spiritual entity to accommodate in Book 8: '*paramam purusham divyam*', the 'divine supreme spirit' or 'divine supreme person', which occurs in 8:8 as the focal point of attention for the *yogin* and at which state he arrives at the moment of death (8:10). The supreme goal, however, is once more and throughout said to be 'me', and very specifically, in 8:21 and 8:22, the 'imperishable' in which the self dwells, and that *this* is the supreme spirit. Since they are both described as the focus of attention and devotion, we must interpret this hyperbolic reference to the 'divine supreme spirit' as one with the supreme self, with 'me', and not as a reference to something else not elsewhere disclosed.

Arjuna's question in 8:2: What happens when you die? initiates a brief summary of the doctrine of the eternal return and how the *yogin*, his attention firmly on the supreme goal, may escape that fate by choosing to follow the way of 'light' to arrive at his true and permanent abode in his original and highest nature, a reward which is said to be far above the merit acquired (towards favourable rebirth) by practising the vedic rites and sacrifices or austerities, the alternative 'dark' path that leads to rebirth and not to liberation.

8:1
the universe in all its power. 'brahman'.

the supreme self. 'adhyatma'.

action. 'karma'.

the supreme spirit. 'adhibhuta'.

God. 'adhidaivata'.

8:2
the highest sacrifice. 'adhiyajna'.

at the hour of death. Arjuna's questions recapitulate the statements in 7:29 and 7:30, but with one subtle shift in emphasis at the end of 8:2. We have learned in 7:30, as also in 2:72, that it is never too late to come to the realisation of the self 'even' at the hour of death. But the formulation of the question now opens up a longer digression on what actually is supposed to happen 'at' the hour of death (just as it might occur in the Christian argument: If I return to God at the hour of death, is my soul saved? and similarly exemplifying the confusion and conflation of the restoration of the soul in God with its fate after death).

8:3
The supreme power. 'Brahman'.

The supreme self. 'Adhyatma'.

and gives rise to them. In the *samkhya* system beings are descended from the supreme sense of pure being degraded into material selfish beings attached to their worldly desires through the action of the *gunas*.

Action. 'Karma'.

8:4
The supreme spirit. 'Adhibhuta'.

God. 'adhidaivata'.

The highest sacrifice. 'Adhiyajna'.

the self embodied here and now. Krishna employs another

epithet (not translated) for Arjuna in this verse: 'O Best of the Embodied', an example of how the epithets used throughout the *Gita* are often formulated to mirror the topic or circumstance: 'the self embodied here and now, O Best of the Embodied'.

The 'technical' terms in verses 8:1-8:4 with the prefix *adhi* are not actually nouns but adverbial forms relating to a sphere of action giving rise to an effect. They can be thought of as metaphysical qualities rather than the functions of separate agencies. We have a universe with a number of aspects or attributes: a sustaining creative power; implicitly transient forms of being that spring from an enduring creative source; an intransient pure consciousness of being; agency or causality – all of which are subsumed here under the one 'me' as the object of devotion whose 'all' (7:19) we are to work towards, having abandoned attachment to our lower selves. To die unrepentant and unenlightened is to start over in another mean existence.

8:7
and fight! We are taken back to the context of the battle in a verse that parallels 3:30, where Arjuna is exhorted to fight by surrendering his actions 'to me'.

8:11
the eternal. We might expect here some difference of view about the aims of these seekers after the 'eternal' and the goal of the *yogin*. But it is clear from the following verses that they are the same.

8:12
yogic concentration. I have retained '*yoga*', '*yogic*' and '*yogin*' as terms where they refer to the commonly understood practice of concentration and breath control and its practitioner.

8:16

As far as the creator's realm. 'Up to the sphere of Brahma [the god of creation].'

8:17

The literal translation of this passage is: 'Those who know that a day for Brahma lasts a thousand *yugas* [a *yuga* here is a period of 4,320,000 years] and that a night for Brahma ends only after a thousand *yugas*, they are men who (truly) know day and night.' We are at this point being introduced to the myth of the eternal return of the universe from its unmanifest form to its subsequent manifestations, a cycle of creation and destruction occurring after a defined period. Apart from the oddness of the exactitude of the periods involved the idea accords well enough with current (unprovable) theories of the constant creation and destruction of multiple universes (where their periodicity is irrelevant, and inconceivable, since time and space are both integral to each universe).

8:20

unmanifest. The primeval unmanifest state is the unmanifest or dormant potential of the universe awaiting its manifest form. The 'higher' umanifest is the supreme self embodied in its perishable bodily form in 'beings'.

8:22

reached only through devotion to it. The longer reading of this line would be 'attained by devotion (to it alone) and not by (devotion to) any other (object of worship)', implying the superiority of the way of *yoga* discipline to other paths.

8:23-8:26

In these verses we see the alignment of the mythical components of this cosmology, of the eternal conflict between light and dark exemplified by the phases of the sun

THE SONG OF MYSELF

and moon, with the way of *yogic* illumination by which the *yogin* is rescued from rebirth, and the dark way by which, if he is to be reborn, his rebirth is accomplished. The modern reader will prefer to see this description of these two mythological journeys of the departed soul as metaphors for choosing the right way over a misguided way, rather than as a manual for choosing the right time of year to die. That this reading may in any case have been meant seems to be borne out in the final two verses of the chapter.

I have not attempted an exegesis of these passages and I have translated them with some freedom in order to render them reasonably intelligible as poetic metaphors. The *Gita* text here has its source in the *Chandogya Upanishad*. The indigenous, non-Aryan (and non-vedic) origins of this mythology are explored by Joseph Campbell in the chapter 'Ancient India' in his *Oriental Mythology*.

The references to fire in 8:24 and to smoke in 8:25 are to the fire and smoke of the cremation in which the dead depart, either in the flame to the sun, from which they do not return, or in the smoke to the moon (to the ancestors), from which they return the way they went – in smoke and mist.

8:27

he. the *yogin*.

8:28

merit. The merit accumulated towards a more providential rebirth. Finally we have the resolution of the 'difference' hinted at in 8:11: the way of *yoga* taught throughout the *Gita* is always superior to other paths.

9

A LEAF, A FLOWER

*I acknowledge the duplicates of myself, the weakest and shallowest is
deathless with me* Walt Whitman, *Song of Myself*

9:1   To you
who show no disrespect
I shall reveal
this utmost secret:
wisdom and its realisation –
and when you understand
you shall be freed from ills.

9:2   This is royal knowledge
and a royal secret,
the pure essence,
plain to see, easy to follow,
true and lasting.

9:3   Men who have no faith in this,
the rule of truth,
do not come to me
but die and are reborn.

9:4   I am unmanifest
and all-pervading
in the universe.
All beings are contained in me
but I am not contained by them.

9:5   And yet they do not dwell in me.

(Behold my mystery and majesty!)
I bear them in myself,
I bring them forth.

9:6   Like the mighty wind
that never fails,
contained within the endlessness of space,
so are beings contained in me.
Reflect on this!

9:7   After a thousand ages
comes the night
when all beings
revert to my material self.
Comes the day,
I send them forth again.

9:8   I send forth
out of my material nature
by my will
this multitude of beings,
for they have no will
themselves.

9:9   And yet their actions
do not bind me.
I sit apart
detached from them.

9:10   I am the eternal witness
and material cause
of all things animate and inanimate
by which the world exists.

9:11   Those who do not know me
as my higher self
despise me in my human form,
ignorant of my lordly being.

9:12   Those unthinking people
       with their vain hopes
       and vain actions
       and worthless knowledge
       live like demons,
       deluded by their very natures.

9:13   But great souls
       shelter in their divine natures
       and have no other thought but me.
       They know me as the origin of all,
       they know me as eternal.

9:14   They praise me always.
       Ever striving, firm of purpose,
       they devote themselves to me.

9:15   Others make the sacrifice of wisdom.
       They, too, worship me
       as the one and as the all,
       for I am everywhere
       and I am many.

9:16   I am the rite
       and I am the sacrifice,
       the offering, the herb,
       the mantra, the ghee.
       I am the fire
       and the pouring out
       into the fire.

9:17   I am the father of this world,
       mother, grandsire, founder,
       the object of all knowledge.
       I am the sanctifier,
       the sacred syllable *OM*,
       and I am the songs of praise
       and their singing.

9:18   I am the means,

the nourisher, the lord
and witness,
a home, a refuge
and a friend.
I am the beginning
and the end
and the enduring,
a hidden treasure,
an immortal seed.

9:19   I am the heat of the sun,
the giver and withholder of the rain.
I am death and deathlessness,
being and nothingness.

9:20   Those versed in the Vedas,
the soma drinkers, the sanctified
who sacrifice to me,
have heaven on their mind
and seek the meritorious world
of the God of gods
where they may enjoy themselves.

9:21   And afterwards,
when that merit is exhausted,
back they come,
re-entering this mortal world
in accordance with the vedic laws
that they themselves invoked.
By getting what they want
they come and go like this.

9:22   But for those who think
only of me
and worship me
and never waver,
I alone
will bring them a possession
they may have and hold.

9:23   Even those who worship other gods
       and sacrifice to them in faith,
       by that faith they worship me
       in fact, if not according to the rule.

9:24   For I am the enjoyer
       and the lord of every sacrifice.
       But they do not know me as I am,
       and so they fall away.

9:25   Those who worship the gods
       go to the gods
       and those devoted to the ancestors
       go to them.
       Those who put their faith in goblins
       have their goblin world,
       but the one who loves me
       comes to me.

9:26   A leaf, a flower,
       a fruit, or water
       I accept
       when offered with devotion
       and a pure heart.

9:27   In all you do,
       in what you eat,
       in whatever offerings you make,
       whatever sacrifice you undertake,
       do them all as offerings to me.

9:28   And you shall come to me,
       through this teaching of renunciation,
       freed from bondage to your actions
       from which both good and evil flow.

9:29   I am the same self in every being
       and neither love one nor despise another.
       Those who offer me devotion

are at one with me, and I with them.

9:30   Even a most evil man
who turns to me devotedly
is thought of as a righteous man
once he has resolved his mind to this.

9:31   He all at once becomes his rightful self
and finds a place of rest,
for none is ever lost who comes to me.

9:32   Those who find in me their refuge,
even those whose origins arise from sin:
women, peasants, servants,
will also reach the highest goal.

9:33   How much easier is it, therefore,
for the priestly class
and our devoted royal seers,
who find themselves abandoned
in this transient and unhappy world.
Devote yourself to me!

9:34   Devote your thoughts to me,
worship me and make your sacrifice to me.
Make me your highest object.
In this never waver
and you yourself will come to me.

NOTES ON THE TEXT AND TRANSLATION

In this chapter Krishna begins by once more promising to reveal the 'royal' secret of the realisation of the self through the understanding and practice of his *yoga* teaching. And once again a line is drawn between that superior teaching leading to realisation and the routine practice of sacred rites whose effects are limited, positioning the supreme self as the ultimate and the only worthwhile goal.

From verse 9:15 where we hear: 'I am everywhere and I am many', the attributes of the self, of the 'I' and the 'me' of this poem, begin to mount up to a catalogue of the 'many' that are contained within the 'one'. It is perhaps at this point that the temptation to see the *Gita* as a theistic work, to translate Krishna into 'God' and the teaching into a question of religious faith, is at its strongest.

The 'I', to quote from another mystical poet, Thomas Traherne, is the 'ring enclosing all' and the 'heavenly eye much wider than the sky'.[1] The 'I' is (in verse 9:10) 'the eternal witness', the same 'I' of Walt Whitman that is 'not contain'd between my hat and boots'.[2] We would be as mistaken to take the 'I' of the *Gita* for God as we would, two thousand years from now in unearthing a battered fragment of *Leaves of Grass*, to take Walt Whitman's assertion that he sees God 'in my own face in the glass'[3] to be anything more than the intuitive realisation of the power of subjective consciousness to sustain – in one person here and now – the whole of phenomenal existence and a universal democracy: 'I am the same self in all beings' (9:29) could be Walt speaking.

Yet though the 'I', the 'self', the *atman* 'brings

[1] Traherne, Thomas. *Centuries of Meditations: The Third Century* in *Selected Poems and Prose*. Harmondsworth: Penguin Books, 1991.

[2] *Song of Myself* (line 133).

[3] *Song of Myself* (line 1285).

forth' all phenomenal manifestations there is always that other 'unmanifest' aspect of the universe that is the unknowable foundation of this self that encloses all. In the *Gita* it is called *brahman*. To find the parallel in western philosophy we need to turn to Kant and the concept of the 'noumenon' (to distinguish the unknowable world in itself from the phenomenal world presented to the mind and the understanding) and to Schopenhauer, following Kant, for whom the thing-in-itself is the Will.

Absent the self and self-consciousness and we assume the world carries on without us, as it was before we came into being, on its own ground as the 'Will' or as *brahman*. But we do not know this directly in experience. It is a deduced fact *in* knowledge but not a realisable knowledge. The only way that the Will can be known, that *brahman* can be comprehended, is *as* the self, as subjectivity. It otherwise remains hidden in its objectivity, without form – yet giving rise to all phenomena. Where do the phenomena created by *brahman* (the 'material cause') actually appear? In the self, in the only sphere of 'being' there is. The self and *brahman* are one. It is *this* realisation that allows the 'I' to speak with such extreme confidence in the *Gita* as the 'one' and the 'all', not as God the creator, manipulator, intervener and external agent, but as the actionless 'witness' through whom all things are accomplished and all things 'animate and inanimate' (9:10) are brought into being.

If the self contains all this, then it is surely entitled, in its flights of poetic imagination, to call itself 'divine'. Given that the realisation of the self is identified as the highest realisable state of being, that all great souls have a divine nature (9:13) and that all beings are 'in me' (9:6), then the 'me', in this context of religious ritual and competing teachings that fall short of the ultimate reward, is surely something to be 'worshipped', not with the object of a reward, but with the gift of 'a leaf, a flower'. Those who understand turn away from the perpetuation of their earthly condition and its impermanent prizes towards the one and the all that does not perish, for it is itself the creator and sustainer of everything. It may, indeed, be 'known as' God (7:30), for what is God if not the absolute of subjectivity freed from the objective condition of the Will?

9:1
This verse has a strong parallel with 7:2.

disrespect. A reference to those who speak ill of or murmur against this doctrine (see 3:31-3:32).

9:2
royal knowledge. Further confirmation of the princely (*kshatriya*) line of descent of this doctrine.

9:4
unmanifest. The unmanifest is that unmanifest identified in 8:20 as 'something higher' and described in 8:22 as lying within all beings and filling the universe.

9:5
The apparent contradiction between 9:4 and 9:5 is resolved in the next verse in the analogy with the wind that is everywhere, contained within the endlessness of space, albeit left as a mystical conundrum to be pondered on.

9:7
After a thousand ages. See 8:17-8:19.

9:11
Those who do not know me...despise me. 'The deluded despise me'. The 'deluded' are the same ones who are blind to this teaching in 3:32, in contrast to Arjuna himself, who is not a

'despiser' or doubter (9:1).

9:12
vain actions. The vain actions of those of vain wisdom or knowledge who pursue the vain 'hopes' of reward from their (ritual) actions, deluded by their own natures, by the *gunas*. We have learned in 2:45 that the Vedas belong to the world of the *gunas*. The verse can be read in conjunction with 7:15.

9:14
firm of purpose. 'steadfast in *yoga*'.

9:15
the sacrifice of wisdom. See 4:33: 'the offering of wisdom is better than material sacrifices'.

for I am everywhere and I am many. 'I am variously manifest as the many and omnipresent.'

9:14 and 9:15 relate to the two 'ways' of the *samkhya*: the way of action (9:14) and the way of wisdom (9:15).

9:16
ghee. 'sacrificial butter'.

the pouring out into the fire. See 4:24: 'and the fire and the pouring out into the fire are also *brahman*'. *Brahman* is the true object of all worship and, ultimately, 'as the one and as the all', of all the vedic rites.

9:17
the songs of praise. Literally, 'the Rig, Sama and Yajur Vedas', the three principal collections of hymns, chants and formulas.

9:20

soma. Formerly, in the early Aryan cults, an intoxicating fermentation of the soma plant.

the sanctified. 'the purified'. Part of the ritual consumption of the dream-inducing soma liquor is its purification through a sieve.

who sacrifice to me. See 9:23-9:24

God of gods. Indra, the chief god of the pantheon.

The rites are always assumed to be effective for their purpose, but that purpose is never, in the *Gita*, considered admirable. These are actions that acquire merit, but do not achieve release.

9:21

And afterwards. 'After having enjoyed the wide world of heaven'.

9:23

This statement is consistent with that first made in 7:21: 'Wherever faith is found and in whatever form it takes, I grant it.'

9:24

they fall away. They fail to recognise the rescuing power of this insight and fall back to earth.

9:25

goblins. 'spirits' or 'ghosts'. Edgerton uniquely gives 'goblins' here, and I have gratefully adopted his choice.

the one who loves me comes to me. 'those who sacrifice to me will come to me.' This verse is an extended version of 7:23.

9:28

through this teaching of renunciation. 'disciplined in the *yoga* of renunciation'.

actions. Actions and, in particular in this context, ritual actions are now subsumed under selfless devotion, with no reward in mind, with the offering of nothing more than 'a leaf, a flower'.

9:29

the same self. The self is the same self in all beings, an impartial entity. Those not devoted to it are not despised by it, but the self is of no avail to those who do not recognise it.

9:32

from sin. The underlying belief is that sinfulness in life leads to rebirth with a lower status in an absolute social hierarchy.

women, peasants, servants. 'Women, *vaishyas* [the third order in the caste system, traders and agricultural workers or peasants], *shudras* [the lowest caste of servants]'. Women, of course, hold a lower social status in this system. The point of this statement is not to disparage any of these classes but simply to recognise, in relation to the 'fine Brahmin' in the next verse, that those born into these lower strata have their own duties (*dharma*) given at birth and do not assume to themselves the *dharma* of another caste (see 3:35), least of all the burden of speculation or religious duties assigned properly to the *brahman* caste, or to the princely *kshatriya* or warrior caste to which the 'royal seers' referred to in 9:33 belong. The self, as we have learned in the preceding verses, is the 'same' in all beings, and while all beings might achieve the ultimate goal, it is harder for the lower orders.

9:33
the priestly class. 'the fine Brahmins'.

devoted royal seers. The implication is, that while the Brahmins should have the intellectual capacity (and the time) to shift their consciousness in the direction of the realisation of the self, the 'royal seers' are already devoted to the idea since they are either of the *samkhya* contemplative school or belong to the school of *karma yoga*, the 'two ways'.

9:34
Make me your highest object. 'intent on me as the supreme object'.

never waver. 'having become steadfast in *yoga* discipline'.

10

THE LORD OF ALL THE WORLD

My ties and ballasts leave me, my elbows rest in sea-gaps,
I skirt sierras, my palms cover continents,
I am afoot with my vision. Walt Whitman, *Song of Myself*

10:1   Hear again from me
       words of the highest import,
       for you are dear to me
       and I care for you.

10:2   The multitude of gods,
       the great seers,
       do not know
       how I came to be.
       The truth is
       they originate with me.

10:3   He who knows me
       as the unborn
       without origin,
       the lord of all the world,
       is undeluded
       in this mortal world
       and hence is free
       from every ill.

10:4   Every condition of being
       arises with me:
       the intellect, its knowledge,
       the enlightened understanding;

forbearance, sincerity,
and equanimity of mind;
happiness and suffering,
birth and death,
fear and fearlessness;

10:5   non-violence, impartiality,
contentment; restraint,
benevolence and reputation,
whether good or bad.

10:6   Where do the legendary seers
and the founders of the human race arise
but in my mind?

10:7   Let there be no doubt
that he who truly knows
the power manifest in me
through yoga is through yoga
unerringly at one with me.

10:8   I am the maker,
everything proceeds from me.
My worshippers are those men
of intelligence who realise this,
who share this state of mind.

10:9   They meditate on me,
think of me and speak of me,
rejoice in me, content
themselves with me
and live their lives for me,
helping each other
towards enlightenment.

10:10   For those who never waver

in their love for me
I teach enlightenment
and the road
by which they come to it.

10:11   Out of compassion for them,
I who live within them,
have one purpose only,
to destroy the darkness
born of ignorance
with wisdom's shining light.

*

10:12   Arjuna spoke and said:
Thou art the Supreme Brahman,
the Highest Abode,
the Supreme Sanctifier,
the Eternal Divine Spirit,
the unborn, all-pervading
Primal God.
10:13   Thus art Thou called
by all the seers,
the divine seer Narada,
Asita Devala and Vyasa.
Now in Thine own Person
dost Thou tell me.
10:14   I believe that all
that Thou hast told to me
is true, O Long-Haired One.
O Blessed One,
not even gods or demons,
know Thy true form.
10:15   Only Thou Thyself knowest Thyself,
O Supreme Spirit, Lord of Beings

and their Creator, God of Gods
and Master of the Universe.

10:16 Now tell me if Thou wilt in full
all the divine forms
in which Thy Self is manifest
throughout the many worlds.

10:17 How may I know Thee, Yogin?
In which form of being
should I think of Thee
and meditate on Thee,
O Blessed One?

10:18 Tell me each and all
Thy many powers and forms
in which, O Krishna, Thou art manifest.
For never will I tire of hearing
Thine ambrosial words.

10:19 The Lord spoke and said:
Let it be so.
But I shall tell you only
of the foremost of my forms divine
in which I manifest myself,
for I am limitless.

10:20 I am the self
abiding in the heart of every being.
I am the beginning
and the middle and the end of all.

10:21 I am Vishnu, chief
among the supreme gods.
Of the stars I am the sun.
I am the chief god of the storm gods
and in the zodiac I am the moon.

10:22 I am the Sama Veda of the Vedas,
I am Indra, chief of all the gods.
Among the senses I am mind,

in beings I am thought.

10:23   I am Shiva of the roaring gods,
Vittesa of the underworld
of sprites and demons.
I am fire among the elemental gods,
and I am Meru, mountain of the middle earth.

10:24   I am first among the priests
and god of war among the generals.
I am the ocean of lakes and seas.

10:25   Among great seers
I am Bhrigu, the greatest of them all.
Of spoken words
I am *OM*,
of offerings
the muttered prayer,
of all that is immovable
I am the Himalayas.

10:26   Of trees I am the sacred fig,
of heavenly seers Narada.
Among celestial musicians
I am Chitraratha,
the heavenly chief of them,
and I am that saintly sage Kapila.

10:27   Know that I am Indra's horse,
born of the churning ocean of ambrosia.
I am the prince of princely elephants
and a king among men.

10:28   I am the thunderbolt of weapons,
the wish-fulfilling cow of cows.
I am the procreating god of lust
and the serpent-king of serpents.

10:29   I am Ananta,
the endless and eternal Worm,
Varuna, water god,
among the monsters of the deep.

Of ancestors am I the chief
and of the doers-down
I am Yama, Death.

10:30　I am the Prince Prahlada
among the demon enemies of God.
I am Time itself
among the reckoners of time.
Of beasts I am the lion, king of beasts,
and of the birds I am the bird Garuda.

10:31　Of all that purifies
I am the purifying wind.
I am Rama
warrior hero of the weapon-bearing.
I am the crocodile
among the monsters of the waters.
I am the Ganges,
the river of rivers.

10:32　I am the beginning of creation
and the middle and the end.
Of all that might be known
I am the knowledge of the supreme self.
I am the speech of those who speak.

10:33　I am the letter A,
the first of letters,
and where two words are joined together
I am that which joins them.
I am the infinity of time
and I am ever present.

10:34　I am all-destroying death,
and I am that which waits upon
all that is yet to be.
I am the feminine nouns
for fame and fortune,
wisdom, speech and constancy,
patience and remembrance.

10:35   I am the melody of the chants,
        the metre of the hymns.
        I am the first month of the year
        and I am spring
        when flowers bloom.

10:36   I am the fateful dicing of the cheats,
        the splendour of the splendid.
        I am victory and perseverance,
        and I am virtue in the virtuous.

10:37   Of the Vrishnis I am Krishna,
        of the Pandus I am Arjuna,
        the sage Vyasa of the sages
        and the poet Ushana of the poets.

10:38   I am the rod the ruler wields,
        the strategist in victory.
        I am the silence of the secretive
        and the wisdom of the wise.

10:39   I am the seed of all that is
        without which nothing can exist.
        All things animate and inanimate
        exist through me.

10:40   There is no end to forms divine
        by which I manifest myself.

        I have told you only this much.

10:41   All that is manifest as glorious
        and filled with power,
        you should understand,
        derives its splendour
        from a fraction of my own.

10:42   But what more could I say to you?
        What more do you need to know?
        The whole world is supported, always,
        by one particle of me.

NOTES ON THE TEXT AND TRANSLATION

With verse 10:11 the largely coherent and consecutive teaching of the *Gita* comes to a natural and satisfying close with a conclusive valedictory address which has many Buddhist parallels. But, beginning with 10:12, this chapter marks an entirely new phase that continues through to the end of Book 11.

We have become accustomed to the framework device of question and answer, with Arjuna, as the acolyte, requesting clarification from Krishna, as *yogin* and teacher, of the tenets and practices of the *karma yoga* school. At the end of Book 9 we left Arjuna being invited once more to take up the true path of *yoga* and to devote himself to the realisation of the supreme self, to 'wisdom and its realisation'. It comes as something of a shock to now find Arjuna transformed from enquiring novice to visionary and fearful worshipper of God in the many divine forms of Vishnu. The 'flowery speech' (see 2:42) in which Krishna is addressed as the incarnation of Vishnu is also in marked contrast to the language of the earlier chapters, and that shift in tone is reflected here in the translation.

There can be little doubt that this section through to the end of Book 11 is a much later component of the *Gita* text as it has come down to us. The natural, and very humanistic conclusion at 10:11 appears to have provided a hiatus in the narrative and the occasion to introduce a later Vaishnava hymn of praise. There is little reference here to the doctrine and the sentiments expressed in the earlier chapters. Rather, the supreme goal, the refuge and abode of the realised self achieved through rigorous discipline and understanding, and the powers of the sustaining principle of *brahman*, are all transposed into attributes of a divine power and a divine being in which the universe itself and the whole pantheon of the vedic gods, the scriptures and the traditional epics are contained. The contrarian doctrine of the royal 'seers' and the *yoga* path of the *samkhya* that leads to enlightenment give way to an orthodox religious doctrine that the 'supreme goal' is a Supreme God, deserving of worship and obeisance.

10:6
The reference is to the 'seven great seers' of legend and the equally legendary 'four Manus', one of whom is mentioned in 4:2. There are supposedly many Manus, the progenitors of the human race, one for each cycle in the destruction and creation of the universe.

10:13
Narada and Asita Devala are legendary composers of some of the hymns of the *Rig Veda*. Vyasa is the legendary compiler of the Vedas and of the *Mahabharata* itself.

10:14
O Long-Haired One. An epithet of Krishna. It has frequently been used in earlier verses but omitted from the translation.

10:20
These two statements succinctly capture the essence of *brahman-atman* but are quickly passed over, and the rest of the chapter concerns itself with the investiture of Krishna/Vishnu as the highest god.

10:21
the supreme gods. 'the Adityas', a group of twelve 'supreme' gods, of whom Vishnu was chief god.

chief god of the storm gods. 'Marici of the Maruts'.

10:22
Sama Veda. Of the three Vedas the *Sama Veda* is the one

which deals with the chants related to the hymns of the *Rig Veda*.

10:23
The verse in full reads: 'Of the Rudras [the 'roaring' gods of creation and destruction] I am Shamkara [Shiva, chief of those gods]. I am Vittesa [also known as Kubera, the lord of wealth and king of the underworld] of the Yakshas and Rakshas [unpredictable imps and sprites]. Of the Vasus [the eight elemental gods] I am Pavaka [another name for Agni, the god of fire, who has appeared earlier in the *Gita*] and among mountains I am Meru [the Mount Olympus of Indian mythology, situated in the middle of the world and whose height exceeds any credible estimation].'

10:24
first among the priests. 'Brihaspati', chief of household priests and priest to the gods.

the god of war. 'Skanda'.

10:26
Kapila. The founder of the *samkhya* school of philosophy.

10:27
Indra's horse. 'Uccaihshravas', Indra's steed, created when the gods churned up the ocean for 'nectar' or ambrosia.

prince of princely elephants. 'Airavata', Indra's elephant.

10:28
thunderbolt. The weapon of Indra.

wish-fulfilling cow. 'Kamahuk', the mythical 'cow of wishes' able to fulfil all desires.

procreating god of lust. 'Kandarpa', known also as Kama, the god of sexual desire.

serpent king. 'Vasuki'.

10:29
Ananta. The unending snake coiled around the world and, like the Worm Ouroborus of Norse mythology, a symbol of eternity. 'Worm' in Old English (*wyrm*) is a serpent or dragon.

Of ancestors am I the chief. 'I am Aryaman'.

doers-down. Refers to the forces of subjugation or instruments of order.

Yama was the first mortal man and thenceforth the god of death.

10:30
Prahlada defected from the Daityas, the 'demon enemies' of the gods, and became a worshipper of Vishnu.

Garuda is the fabled bird and 'vehicle' of Vishnu.

10:31
Rama. The warrior hero of the *Ramayana* and an incarnation of Vishnu.

10:33
where two words are joined together. Words, among the Brahmins, as elsewhere, had magical powers. To master words and their compounds was to master the gods and the way to them. To make an error in grammar is to mistake the coherence of the world itself. Witness Gandhi's mortification

on splitting a Sanskrit vowel combination on the first day of his talks on the *Gita*: 'I displayed my ignorance, not knowledge.'[1]

10:35
the melody of the chants, the metre of the hymns. The verse refers specifically to the chants to Indra in the *Sama Veda* and to the unique metre of the *Rig Veda*.

10:36
I am the fateful dicing of the cheats. 'I am the gambling of the cheats'. There has been much discussion of the meaning of this line, and why 'gambling' appears here at all. It may mean to express the idea that, since God determines all outcomes, like the cheat at gambling, nothing happens by chance. Dicing featured prominently in the culture of the time. There is a prayer for success at dice in the *Atharva Veda* (7.50), and the snares of dice are the subject of a whole hymn in the *Rig Veda* (10.34).

10:37
Krishna. 'Vasudeva' in the text, the patronymic of Krishna of the Vrishni clan. In its urgency to equate Krishna (Vishnu) with the first in all categories, and to associate his divinity with the founding texts of the vedic religion and with the epics, the catalogue of identities goes so far as to include Krishna himself and Arjuna as hero of the epic *Mahabharata*, as well as the legendary sage/poet Vyasa, the reputed author of the Vedas, the *Mahabharata* and the *Gita* itself.

10:42
one particle of me. This claim, and its expression in the previous verse as a 'fraction', should not be taken as a metaphysical

---

[1] Gandhi, 1926

idea suggesting the fragmentation of the 'supreme self', but simply as a further example of hyperbole in describing the ways in which Vishnu exhibits his power and prowess. The 'self' and the sustaining principle of the universe (*brahman*) in the core doctrine are always a unity, present in all but not in the sense of being divided up and distributed among all.

11

IF A THOUSAND SUNS SHOULD RISE

Divine am I inside and out Walt Whitman, *Song of Myself*

11:1 Thou hast spoken out of kindness to me
and revealed to me
the highest mystery,
the supreme self,
and I am freed from my delusions.

11:2 I have heard from Thee in every detail,
O Lotus-Petal-Eyed,
of the origin and dissolution of all beings
and of Thine own Eternal Majesty.

11:3 As Thou hast described Thyself,
so I wish to see Thee,
Supreme Spirit,
in Thy form divine.

11:4 If Thou deemst it possible,
O Lord and Prince of Yoga,
to see Thee as Thou art,
reveal to me Thine own Eternal Self.

11:5 Behold my heavenly forms
a hundred-fold. Nay, a thousand-fold
in various shapes and colours.

11:6 Behold the many wonders
of the universe never seen before:
the supreme deities themselves,
the elemental gods, the roaring gods,
the twin celestial horsemen of the dawn,

the gods of storm and thunder,
11:7   and all things moving and immovable
contained entirely in my body.
What else would you like to see?
11:8   But with your own eyes you can't see me.
Therefore I bestow on you
a divine eye.
And now behold me
in my power and majesty!

11:9   Sanjaya spoke and said:
O King, thus having spoken,
the mighty Lord of Yoga, Hari Krishna,
revealed to him His supreme form
in all its majesty.

11:10   Many mouths and many eyes
he had and many other marvels,
ornaments and armaments divine
lifted up on high, wearing
11:11   divine garlands and divine garments,
divine perfumes and ointments:
an infinite all-seeing god
made of many marvels.
11:12   If a thousand suns should rise at once
the splendour of that Great One
would be like the splendour of that sky.
11:13   Then Arjuna beheld
the many in the one,
the universe embodied
in the God of Gods.
11:14   He was amazed.
His hair stood up on end.
Reverently he bowed before the God
and said:

11:15 I see the gods embodied
in Thy Body, all of them,
of every kind, O God.
Brahma on his lotus-seat,
and all the seers
and all the heavenly serpents.

11:16 And Thou hast many arms
and bellies, mouths and eyes.
I see Thee, Lord of All,
in infinite directions,
whose form has no beginning,
middle nor an end
but is the Form of All,

11:17 with crown and sceptre,
carrying the discus.
I see Thee as a mass of splendour
shining on all sides,
so hard to look upon
the infinite brilliance
of Thy sun-like fire.

11:18 Thou art the imperishable
supreme object of all knowledge,
the highest place of rest,
the original primeval spirit,
the indestructible defender of eternal law.
Thus do I believe.

11:19 Thy power has no beginning,
middle nor an end.
Thine arms are many, Thine eyes
the sun and moon.
Behold, I see Thy sacrifice-consuming
mouth of fire and see the universe
ablaze with Thine own brilliance.

11:20 Heaven and earth are filled
with Thee alone, Exalted One,

and at Thy wondrous form most terrible
the three worlds tremble.

11:21 There the throngs of gods process before Thee,
some in fear with reverence praise Thee.
Throngs of seers and those
who have achieved perfection
hail Thee, praise and magnify Thee.

11:22 All of them behold Thee in amazement:
the Rudras, Adityas, Vasus and the Sadhyas,
the Vishve deities, the Ashvins
and the Ushmapas, the Yakshas, Gandharvas,
Asuras and perfected ones in throngs.

11:23 Thy form is great, with many mouths and eyes,
and many-armed, O Mighty-Armed One.
Many thighs and feet and terrifying fangs Thou bearest.
Worlds tremble at Thy sight. And so do I.

11:24 Thou reachest to the sky in blazing colours,
with yawning jaws agape and blazing eyes.
Seeing Thee I tremble in my heart, O Vishnu,
finding neither peace nor courage there.

11:25 Beholding Thee with terrifying fangs
and yawning mouths
burning like the fires of all-consuming time,
I have no place to turn for refuge.
Have mercy on me, Lord of Gods,
Home of the Universe.

11:26 There the sons of Dhritarashtra,
all the kings, and Bhishma, Drona, Karna
and our chief warriors too,

11:27 rush into Thy gaping jaws of terrifying fangs
where some I see
with heads crushed between Thy teeth.

11:28 Like rivers flow in torrents to the sea,
so the heroes of the world
flow in tongues of flame to Thee.

11:29   As moths consume themselves in flame,
       as quickly do the worlds the same,
       destroyed at once by entering Thy mouths
11:30   that lick and swallow and devour
       them all in flame that lights the universe, O Vishnu,
       with terrible and fiery splendour.
11:31   Tell me who Thou art, so terrible of form.
       Hail to Thee, O Best of Gods. Have mercy on me.
       I wish to know Thee as Thou art
       since time began for yet
       I do not understand Thy works.

11:32   I am Time
       the great destroyer
       come to bring an end to all.
       These warriors in opposing ranks
       shall cease to be
       no matter what transpires.
11:33   Stand up! Seek glory!
       Conquer your enemies and enjoy
       dominion and prosperity.
       For I have struck them down already,
       and you are but the means.
11:34   Drona, Bhishma, Jayadratha, Karna
       and the other warrior heroes I have slain.
       Do not falter. Kill them!
       Fight! And you shall conquer
       your enemies in battle.

11:35   Sanjaya spoke and said:
       Having heard these words of Krishna,
       Arjuna in veneration, trembling,
       bowed before Him, terrified,
       and stammered out these words:

11:36   Rightly doth the world rejoice,
        delighting in Thy praise.
        The demons flee before Thee
        terrified. And shall not all
        perfected ones bow down before Thee?
11:37   Why should they not bow down before Thee,
        O Great God? For Thou art the Creator,
        greater yet than Brahma,
        O Infinite God of Gods, Home of the Universe,
        O Thou who art eternal and beyond
        all that is and shall be.
11:38   Thou art the founding God,
        the primal Universal Spirit
        in which the world abides.
        Thou art the knower and the known
        and highest goal of knowledge,
        pervading all the universe,
        O Thou of Infinite Form.
11:39   Thou art the gods of wind and death,
        the gods of fire and water.
        Thou art the moon,
        Creator Lord of All
        and the world's first Ancestor.
        All hail to Thee, a thousand times!
        All hail! All hail!
11:40   All hail before Thee and behind Thee,
        all hail around Thee!
        Immeasurable in might and valour
        art Thou, O All, for Thou fulfillest all
        and therefore art Thou All!
11:41   If I have addressed Thee in the past
        as Krishna and as comrade,
        forgive me for my ignorance
        of Thy great majesty.
11:42   Or if in friendship or affection

I joked or treated Thee with disrespect
at play or resting or while sitting
or when dining, alone or in the presence
of another, forgive me this, O Boundless One.

11:43 Thou art the Father of the World,
of all things animate and inanimate,
revered by all, a venerable teacher.
None other is there like to Thee
in all three worlds. How could there be
another greater than Thou art,
O Peerless Being?

11:44 And so I bow to Thee,
prostrate myself before Thee
and ask of Thee forgiveness
as of a father to his son,
a friend towards a friend,
a lover to his well-beloved.
O God have mercy on me
if it pleaseth Thee.

11:45 Joyful am I to have seen
that which never has been seen
by any man before.
But yet I tremble.
Let me see that form again,
O God, Thou hadst before.
Have mercy on me, Lord of Gods,
in whom the universe abides.

11:46 Let me see Thee in Thy crown,
bearing the sceptre and the discus,
in Thy four-armed form,
O Thousand-Armed and Form of All.

11:47 By my grace and power
has my supreme form been shown to you,

splendid, infinite, embracing all
since time began and never seen before
by any, saving you.

11:48 Not by vedic sacrifice
or chants or gifts, and nor
by rituals or austerities
can I be seen by anyone
but you, O Hero of the Kurus.

11:49 Be not afraid! Be not disturbed
on seeing this most terrible of forms.
Once more be free from fear.
Take heart, and see me in this form!

11:50 Sanjaya spoke and said:
The Great One having spoken
then revealed once more
His human form, gentle and handsome,
calming Arjuna's fears.

11:51 Arjuna spoke and said:
Now I see Thee in Thy gentle human form,
my mind composed once more,
my heart returned to normal.

11:52 This form of mine,
revealed to you,
is hard to see.
Even the gods
long to behold it.

11:53 Not by vedic lore, by sacrifice,
austerities and gifts
can I be seen as you have seen me,

11:54 but only by unwavering devotion
can I be known and seen and reached.

*

11:55   He who acts in me,
holds me as his highest object
and devotes himself to me,
abandoning attachment,
free from enmity to anyone,
will come to me.

NOTES ON THE TEXT AND TRANSLATION

11:1

The idea of a sudden divine revelation of the 'highest mystery' conveyed in the words of Krishna is in marked contrast to the disciplined, and quite difficult, journey of *yoga* earlier advocated and upon which, when we left him at the end of Book 9, Arjuna is yet to embark. We may take this as confirmation that we are dealing with a somewhat different work distinct from the main body of the *Gita* and its teaching. In this chapter, the concept of self-realisation through the acquisition of knowledge and disciplined practice towards its realisation gives way to the idea of a vision granted at once by divine grace. In fact what has been revealed is not the 'highest mystery', the 'utmost secret' of knowledge and its realisation (*jnana* and *vijnana*) referred to in 9:1, but instead the 'power and majesty' (11:8) of Krishna as the avatar of Vishnu, the 'God of Gods'.

11:2

O Lotus-Petal-Eyed. An epithet of Krishna.

11:6

the supreme gods. 'Adityas'.

the elemental gods. 'Vasus'.

the roaring gods. 'Rudras', the gods of creation and destruction.

the twin celestial horsemen. 'Ashvins', the heralds of dawn.

the storm gods. 'Maruts', the gods of storm and thunder.

11:9

Sanjaya is unexpectedly reintroduced at this point in the role of 'seer', addressing the King Dhritarashtra, as a necessary device to provide the third person narrative description that follows. The vision of the divine forms of Krishna is vouchsafed solely to Arjuna (so stated in 11:47). But to facilitate the description of that vision Sanjaya is recalled to serve as the privileged witness, with his all-seeing eye and overview of the whole of the Kurukshetra story.

Hari is another name for the incarnation of Vishnu.

11:14
His hair stood up on end. A common conventional expression in the *Gita* that accompanies amazement (see 1:29 and 18:74).

11:15
Brahma. Brahma the creator god of the trinity of gods (Brahma, Shiva and Vishnu).

11:20
the three worlds. Heaven, earth and the aether.

11:22
The Rudras, Adityas, Vasus, the Ashvin twins and the Maruts have been cited before (11:16). The Sadhyas are minor deities inhabiting the aether. The Vishve *devas* embody a number of abstract virtues. Ushmapas ('steam-drinkers') are a group of ancestors supposed to consume the steam rising from the food ceremonially offered to them. Asuras are demon enemies of the gods. For Yakshas see 10:23, for Gandharvas see 10:26. I have left all these entities untranslated to illustrate the extent to which this segment of the *Gita* is wedded to the vedic religion and its mythological heritage, with Krishna/Vishnu elevated to the supreme god of the pantheon.

11:23

O Might-Armed One. An epithet of Arjuna used (but not translated) throughout the *Gita*, but here attached to Krishna, purely for poetic effect. It is one of numerous places in the poem where the euphonious conjunction of syllables (in this line, *mahabaho bahubahu*) shapes the verse.

11:32

no matter what transpires. 'even without you', that is, irrespective of the actions of Arjuna in the battle.

11:34

Jayadratha. A king on the Kurava side in the war.

Karna. 'Son of the charioteer', a hero and the adopted son of Adhiratha, charioteer to King Dhritarashtra, mentioned in 1:8. He was later killed by Arjuna in the Kurukshetra war.

There are obvious parallels in verses 11:32-11:34 with verses in Book 2 set on the field of battle, which Book 11 revisits. But whereas in Book 2 the situation presented a platform for Krishna, as teacher, to explain the nature of the self detached from intentional action, and of time the destroyer *sub specie aeternitatis*, here there is no philosophical or reflective context, only its echo as Arjuna is urged to fight, this time not because he has been asked to understand the detached nature of the self and his actions as duty (*dharma*), but because the god Vishnu has sanctioned his worldly ambitions with a distorted form of the same reasoning.

11:37

Brahma. The creator god Brahma. By assigning the role of supreme 'Creator' to Vishnu we need immediately to be told of the subordinate role of Brahma, the creator god of the trinity whose power is here being usurped (see 11:15).

eternal and beyond all that is and shall be. 'the eternal, the existing, the not-existing and that which is beyond both.'

11:39
the gods of wind and death. 'Vayu' and 'Yama'.

the gods of fire and water. 'Agni' and 'Varuna'.

11:46
Krishna is asked to return to his usual self, but there is no precedent elsewhere in the poem for this 'usual' four-armed form with crown, sceptre and discus, which are attributes of the revealed god Vishnu (11:17) and the form in which Vishnu is worshipped. This form is not compatible with the 'human' form in which Krishna is said to reappear in 11:50.

11:48
O Hero of the Kurus. An epithet of Arjuna. Book 11 is very much set in the context of the conflict on the Kuru field. Here, the supreme state of being that is to be acquired by insight rather than accumulated merit (8:28) has been transformed into a vision granted solely by the 'grace and power' (11:47) of God on the field of battle.

11:55
This final, isolated verse returns us, after a long and wild deviation from the doctrine, to the main theme where we left off at the conclusion of Book 9. It rounds off this interlude by emulating the last verse (9:34) of that chapter.

12

O THEY ARE DEAR TO ME

And these tend inward to me, and I tend outward to them...
Walt Whitman, *Song of Myself*

12:1 Which of these
      has the better knowledge of the way:
      those who steadfastly devote themselves to you
      and worship you,
      or those who do the same towards
      that which is eternal and unmanifest?

12:2 Those who always have me in their minds,
      are always steadfast in their worship,
      those of supreme faith,
      are to be thought of as the most attached to me.

12:3 But they, too, come to me
      who worship the imperishable,
      the unmanifest, the indefinable,
      the all-pervading, the unthinkable,
      that which never changes,
      never wavers, the constant and eternal,

12:4 those who have controlled the multitude of senses,
      those of equanimity of mind,
      delighting only in the welfare of all beings.

12:5 The effort is much greater
      for those who fix their minds on the unmanifest,
      for the goal of the unmanifest
      in this life is hard to reach.

12:6 But those surrendering their acts to me,

holding me to be their highest object,
unwavering in discipline,
who think of me alone, who worship me,
12:7 whose thoughts abide in me:
in a while I will deliver them
from the sea of life and death.

12:8 Keep me only in your thoughts,
turn your will to me,
and without doubt
you shall dwell in me hereafter.

12:9 If you cannot keep your mind
steadily on me,
then seek me
through the practice of the discipline.

12:10 And even if you cannot practice this,
act in me, act solely for my sake,
and you shall reach perfection.

12:11 And if even this you cannot do,
find your strength in me
and, abandoning attachment
to the things that you desire,
act in all things with restraint.

12:12 Peace comes with renunciation
more readily than from meditation,
from meditation more certainly than knowledge,
from knowledge much more surely than from practice.

12:13 These are they most dear to me,
the most devoted:
He who does not harbour hatred

but is friendly and compassionate to all,
unattached to notions of the self
and what belongs to him,
patient and enduring,
indifferent to pain and pleasure,

12:14   contented always in himself,
firm in his resolve
to fix his mind and will on me.

12:15   He by whom the world is not disturbed
yet does not shun the world,
released from happiness, impatience,
anxiety and fear

12:16   and expectations. An honest man
and capable, disinterested,
unperturbed, pursuing nothing,

12:17   who neither loves one thing
nor hates another,
who has no sorrows, no desires,
dismissing both the pleasant and unpleasant,

12:18   the same towards an enemy as a friend,
alike in attitude towards a good name or a bad,
the same in heat and cold, in pain and pleasure,

12:19   detached, indifferent to praise or blame,
content with anything,
at home without a home,
silent, imperturbable.

12:20   Those who, in faith, revere
the nectar of these truths
I have declared,
those devoted to me
as their highest object,
O they are dear to me,
so dear to me!

NOTES ON THE TEXT AND TRANSLATION

In verses 9:4 to 9:6 Arjuna was asked to reflect on the nature of the unmanifest: 'I am unmanifest and all-pervading in the universe'. Book 12 is a continuation of Book 9, which ended with the injunction to Arjuna to 'devote yourself to me' (9:33) and to make 'me' the 'highest object' to be worshipped with devotion. Arjuna, as Krishna's questioner, draws out these objects of worship into two strands: Krishna as the personal object of worship, and the 'unmanifest' as the impersonal aspect of that object. Krishna confirms the differentiation in his responses, and we are then introduced to *'bhakti'* or the 'devotional' path. While devotion has already been introduced at 9:14 and is prevalent throughout that chapter, no specific differentiation has been made between the 'me' of the sacrifice or object of worship and the doctrine itself as the highest goal. They are one and the same but, by constant iteration, 'devotion' of itself, as something of value in its own right, has by the end of that chapter become a practical and recommended way of action, with or without a complete understanding; it is of value even in the absence of the rigorous practice of *yoga*, and recommended (9:32) for women, peasants and servants: 'Those who offer me devotion are at one with me, and I with them.' (9:29)

12:1
the way. '*yoga*'.

12:4
delighting only in the welfare of all beings. This (Buddhist influenced) statement appears also in 5:25.

12:5
in this life. 'by embodied beings', i.e. by individual souls.

12:6
surrendering their acts to me. There is some common ground here with 3:30. That earlier verse also occurred in the context of a knowledge appropriate to 'one who knows' and 'one who does not know', who is to be allowed to follow his attachment to acts of worship.

discipline. 'yoga'.

12:7
the sea of life and death. 'the ocean of death and rebirth'.

12:8
your will. 'buddhi'.

12:9
the discipline. 'yoga'

12:10
act in me. 'hold my work as the highest object' – 'my work' (*matkarma*) having been established in Book 3 as acting without attachment to sustain the order of the world.

The doctrinal references here are to 'surrendering their acts to me' (12:6), that is, firstly, to acting without attachment to motives of self-interest; and, secondly, to the act of worship that is 'the only action that is free' (3:9) in which the worshipper acts selflessly 'for my sake'.

12:11
the things that you desire. 'the fruits of action'.

The instruction in 12:11 is similar to that in 12:10, but clearly implies a weakened resolve. The 'lowest' level of practice is reliance on devotion and, rather than acting 'in' or 'for' the unattached higher self that is the 'me' of 12:10, the devotee is asked to act with restraint, with self-control, and not to seek always his own self-interests. It adds up to a general attitude of godliness and goodness in contrast to disciplined practice, effort and understanding.

12:12

This is an extremely problematic verse, the difficulties of which translators and interpreters have either passed over or by their own admission failed to resolve. My own thoughts are no more secure than theirs. At first glance the verse appears to be a summary of the hierarchy of difficulty in the methods of practice enquired into and proposed from 12:1 to 12:11. But on closer reading the literal translation is contradictory and hard to make sense of. This is a literal translation:

> *Knowledge, it is true, is better than practice.*
> *Meditation is superior to knowledge.*
> *Renunciation of the fruits of action is superior to meditation,*
> *for peace soon follows from renunciation.*

'Knowledge' is '*jnana*', which I have translated as 'wisdom' when it is related to the *samkhya* 'two ways' or approaches to self-realisation. 'Practice' can mean 'ritual practice', and throughout the *Gita* wisdom (*jnana-yoga*) has always been held up as superior to adherence to vedic rites. But I think the two complementary schools of the *samkhya* are meant here, and since the 'practice' of the *yoga* discipline has been urged to achieve that understanding, then wisdom as the goal is logically better than the practice itself. The two ways are identified in 3:3. The contrast between them, put simply, is this: in the 'pure' *yoga* of wisdom the practitioner turns his back on the world, but in the *yoga* of action (*karma-yoga*) he continues to act in the world but detached from 'the fruits of action'. It is the peace that arises from this act of renunciation that this verse is leading into.

'Meditation' is an integral part of the 'practice', so it is difficult to see what makes it 'superior' to knowledge or wisdom. In the current context, meditation could be equated with the recommendation in 12:8 to 'keep me only in your thoughts' and therefore with devotion. 'Renunciation' is urged in 12:11, but it is clearly identified as the lowest or weakest of the practices in terms of difficulty of application, and therefore hardly 'superior' to the rest. The hierarchy as given in 12:12 is therefore:

renunciation > meditation > knowledge > (yoga) practice

Some of the difficulties in this statement are resolved if we take the subject, which here as elsewhere in the *Gita* is given at the end of the verse, to be 'peace' or tranquillity of mind, which has often been offered as the prize of renunciation (notably in 2:65 onwards in the earliest section devoted to the *Gita* doctrine). If this is, in this chapter on devotion, what we are being asked to work towards, clearly there is a hierarchy of difficulty, and that hierarchy has been given in the immediately preceding verses. If we put the subject, 'peace', at the beginning and then interpret 'better than' or 'superior to' to mean 'better for you' or 'more fitting' in ease of practice (particularly for the layman who is never going to subject himself to the required discipline) things fall into place and we can see that renunciation would be a 'better' alternative for peace of mind to the acquisition of wisdom and the effort of practice required to achieve it. The peace that comes from this equanimity of mind is the subject of all that follows in the remainder of the chapter.

12:16

pursuing nothing. 'relinquishing all undertakings'.

12:19

at home without a home. Usually translated simply as 'homeless' and often readily taken to indicate a wandering mendicant, which would be incompatible with one who 'does not shun the world' in 12:15. I have taken it to mean at home in the world under any circumstances.

13

THE WITNESS

I witness and wait. Walt Whitman, *Song of Myself*

13:0   Now I wish to know
        what is meant by material nature
        and what is meant by spirit.
        What is the field,
        and the knower of the field,
        knowledge and its object.

13:1   We say this body is the field,
        and that which knows it
        is the knower of the field.

13:2   Understand, I am the knower
        of all fields.
        True knowledge is to know
        the field and know the knower.

13:3   Briefly learn from me
        the nature of this field,
        its changeability and how that comes about,
        and who the knower is
        and what his power is.

13:4   Seers have often sung of this,
        and it is well-defined and reasoned
        in the sacred texts:
13:5   the great elements,

the ego-self,
the intellect,
primal matter,
the ten organs of sensation
plus the mind,
and the five senses,

13:6   desires and aversions,
pain and pleasure,
mind and body
and its resilience.
These things, in brief,
describe the nature of the field,
its moods and modes.

13:7   To be without pride
and free from insincerity,
to embrace non-violence,
patience, virtue and integrity,
constancy and self-restraint,
to attend to his teacher,

13:8   disdaining objects of the senses,
egoless,
always mindful of the evils that arise
from pain, birth, old age, disease and death,

13:9   to be detached, not clinging
to son or wife or home etcetera,
but, constant in an even-minded attitude
to all that might transpire,
desirable or undesired,

13:10   to devote himself to me wholeheartedly,
seeking out a quiet place
to practise yoga single-mindedly,
disillusioned with the company of men –

13:11   this, we say, is wisdom,
to know the highest self

and never fall from it,
to seek the truth of knowledge
in one's heart,
for all that is not this is otherwise.

13:12   But let me tell you
what it is that must be known
by which you come to your immortal state:
it is the highest all-sustaining being,
we say, without beginning,
that is not being
but nor is it non-being.

13:13   Present everywhere throughout the world,
it spreads its hands and feet,
its eyes and ears
and heads and faces
everywhere

13:14   as though possessing
passions and the senses,
though really free from them,
sustaining all without attachment to them,
merely the perceiver of them.

13:15   It lies outside
and inside every being,
animate and inanimate.
It is both near and far,
and for this subtlety
it can't be known.

13:16   Nor is it divided up in beings,
though it appears to be,
being shared by each.
This that must be known
is their sustainer, their creator
and that which reabsorbs them.

13:17   It is the light of lights

beyond the reach of darkness.
This that must be known
is both the goal of knowledge
and that very knowledge,
dwelling in the hearts of all.

13:18   And so you have it. Briefly
I've explained to you
the field,
knowledge itself,
and the object of that knowledge.
My devotee who understands this
lights upon my state of being.

13:19   Know material nature
and the nature of the immaterial
have no beginning,
that the moods and motions
and the temperaments
have material origins.

13:20   Matter is the cause,
the instrument and agent;
the immaterial
the experiencer of pain and pleasure.

13:21   It is this immaterial resident
in the material
that experiences the temperaments
which have material causes.
And it is attachment to these temperaments
that is the cause of cyclic birth,
for good or ill.

13:22   This, the body's highest

immaterial resident,
is called the witness or observer,
the permitter, the supporter,
the experiencer,
the greater ruler and the supreme self.

13:23 He who knows about the immaterial
and knows material nature and its temperaments,
in whatever state of being he possesses
is not born again.

13:24 Some realise the self within the self
by meditation,
others through the discipline of knowledge,
others following the discipline of action.
13:25 Yet there are others
who do not know it,
but having heard of it
dedicate themselves devotedly
to that which they have heard.
They too pass over death.

13:26 Know also, all things that are born
into existence, both animate
and inanimate, are born
from union of the field
with the knower of the field.

13:27 He who sees, sees, who sees
the supreme ruler
as the same in every being,
the everlasting in the transient form.
13:28 And since he sees
the supreme ruler everywhere
he cannot harm the self

by any action of the self,
and thus attains the highest goal.

13:29　He who sees, sees, who sees
all actions are the work
of his material nature
and this alone.
The self does nothing.

13:30　He has attained that supreme state
who sees the various states and modes of being
at rest within the one,
spread out before him.

13:31　This eternal supreme self
has no beginning,
and even though it sits within the body
does not act
and is not tainted
by the temperaments and passions.

13:32　Just as all-pervading space
remains untouched
by virtue of its subtlety,
the omnipresent self
that dwells within the body
is equally unmarred.

13:33　Just as the sun
illuminates the world
in its entirety,
so does the owner of the field
illuminate the field entirely.

13:34　They attain that highest state
who with the eye of wisdom know
the knower of the field
and how it differs from the field itself
and thus how beings are released
from their material nature.

NOTES ON THE TEXT AND TRANSLATION

Book 13 is the clearest explanation we will be given of the essence of the *Gita* doctrine on the relationship between the self as the subject that knows, what it seeks to know, the nature of that knowledge and the material field in which it acts as witness. It is based on the tenets of the *samkhya* system of cosmogony and its theory of being.

It distinguishes objective material nature (*prakriti*) from the immaterial subjective sense of being (*purusha*), the equivalent of the 'soul' of Plato or 'spirit' of Descartes (*purusha* is literally the 'person' that is not the personal ego and the qualities it possesses, which are all properties of *prakriti*). The ego-self and its actions are firmly located in material nature and the *gunas*. That ego-self and its body are referred to as the 'field', and the higher self as the 'knower of the field'. We are taken back to some of the initial statements in Book 2, in which the imperishable self that does not act is distinguished from the material form of the self that acts at the insistence of its material nature through the agency of the *gunas*, and it becomes clear once more that this non-acting 'supreme self' (*paramatman*) is to be identified with non-acting, all-pervasive and sustaining *brahman* that is the goal or object of knowledge (*jneya*) even though it cannot be known directly (13:15). The clarity and concision of this chapter should help illuminate some of the conceptual difficulties encountered in the more prolix, composite and confusing sections of the *Gita*.

But this book, too, has its own disparate components. It begins as an exposition of the elements of the *samkhya* philosophy. The description in 13:6 of the 'field' leads into a brief section on the ideal man and the practice of *yoga* to subdue some aspects of that field (the material body) and its changeable moods and states of mind. 13:12 introduces '*brahman*' as the object of knowledge and then, at 13:19, the lecture picks up the theme of *prakriti* and *purusha*, and the distinction between the field and the knower of the field, concluding at the end of the chapter with a definitive statement that it is the understanding of this separation of the subjective ruler or 'lord' from the given objective condition of one's material nature that is the end and aim of knowledge.

13:0
This verse is absent from some versions of the text. Where included in other translations it is not numbered.

The technical terms, all from the *samkhya* school, are:
prakriti – material nature.
purusha – spirit, soul or 'person', that is, one's non-physical sense of being. (See 13:19 for a fuller discussion.)
kshetra – literally 'field', used in a similar way to our expressions 'field of knowledge', 'field of action' etc., here identified as the material body (which includes the mind) as an object of knowledge.
kshetrajna – the knower of the field.
jnana – knowledge.
jneya – the object of knowledge or, as I have translated it in later verses, 'that which must be known'.

13:1
We say. 'It is said' and 'said by those who know about these things'; that is, by the proponents of the *samkhya* school.

Here, we are simply separating the body as the 'field' and *object* of knowledge from the (non-material) subjective knower embodied in it.

13:2
The 'I' that is the 'knower' here is the 'self' that is common

to all 'fields', that is present in all embodied beings (see 6:29 and 9:29). In our everyday knowledge of ourselves, the field (our body and mind with its thoughts, motives, desires, emotions and its 'knowledge') *is* the self. But true knowledge is knowledge of the abiding subjective self that understands the field of the everyday self and its material nature, and stands above it.

13:4

in the sacred texts. 'in the *brahmasutras*', those texts (their identity is uncertain) that speak aphoristically of *brahman*, indicating a long tradition and historical authority for what follows.

13:5-13:6

These are all elements of the *samkhya* system, which has a hierarchy of creation from undifferentiated primal matter (*prakriti*) descending through the intelligence to the individuated ego, the five 'subtle' elements (the objects of the five senses: sight, hearing, touch, taste, smell) which in turn produce the five 'great' or gross elements. Thence the five senses and their five sensations, a five further 'organs of action' to be added to those, and then the 'mind' or 'heart' through which these sensations are channelled. The final element (the 25th) is the *purusha*, the spirit or singularity of the self in subjective consciousness, which completes the catalogue of the nature of being. These are all given in 13:5, but not in descending order (the order has been dictated by the metrical structure of the verse), except '*purusha*', which is not an element of the 'field' but the 'knower of the field'.

Verse 13:6 captures (briefly, as it says) the elements of the natural will (which will be explored in greater depth in the treatise on the *gunas* in Book 14), its attachment to life, and its emotional engagement with its own interests of power and survival ('resilience'), with which the disengaged self is contrasted in the ensuing verses.

The great elements. The five 'gross' elements of earth, air, fire, water and the aether.

the ten organs of sensation. The eye (light), the ear (sound), the skin (touch), the tongue (taste), the nostrils (odour), plus the five 'organs of action': hand, foot, mouth, anus, penis.

the five senses. Light, sound, touch, taste, smell.

its resilience. The capacity of the organism as a whole to sustain itself.

its moods and modes. Its capacity for change, its changeability.

13:8
pain, birth, old age, disease and death. This purely Buddhist description of the 'wheel of birth and death' has not occurred in exactly this form before.

13:11
for all that is not this is otherwise. 'what is otherwise to this is not-knowledge (ignorance)'.

13:12
the highest all-sustaining being. '*brahman*'.

13:13
In this metaphor we may, perhaps, have the seed of all that was extravagantly developed in Book 11.

13:14
passions. 'the *gunas*'.

13:15
it can't be known. It (*brahman*) can't be known directly. Only the 'field' that is the body and the 'knower of the field' can be known. The knower of the field is the witness, the perceiver, the experiencer, the self, the subjective will and the only form in which *brahman* can be known, or can know itself.

13:17
beyond the reach of darkness. See the parallel in 8:9.

This that must be known. The 'object of knowledge' is bundled with the goal of knowledge and knowledge, or wisdom, itself. We have seen in numerous places in the *Gita* that all three aspects of this wisdom are commended as 'goals': the way or discipline of knowledge, either as *jnana-yoga* (following the *samkhya* teaching) or as *karma-yoga* (the discipline or *yoga* of action taught in the *Gita*); the realisation of knowledge (*vijnana*); and knowledge as the 'highest goal' whose object is the 'supreme self' or the 'me' the adept enters into or becomes one with. The unity of the object of knowledge, knowledge, and the goal reached through knowledge is expressed in the Sanskrit text in this verse as: *jnanam jneyam jnanagamyam.* Not for the first time, we find that any attempt to seek an over-analytical distinction between numerous interchangeable terms is confounded by the priority given to the sound values of the verse.

13:18
And so you have it. 'Thus'. The teacher has not, however, addressed the nature of the 'knower of the field' promised in 13:3. This is taken up in the remaining section of the chapter.

lights upon. 'enters into', 'arrives at'.

13:19
material nature. 'prakriti'.

the immaterial. 'purusha'. Although *'purusha'* has been seen
before in the literal sense of a 'person', and also with its
qualifiers as the 'supreme' or 'divine' person or being,
'purusha' here refers to the immaterial spiritual monad
of the *samkhya* system. As we have indicated before (see
Notes to 7:4 and 7:5), in this system the perishable forms of
matter are descended from undifferentiated primal matter,
to which they return; and the 'being' of beings, which is
immaterial, is descended from *purusha*, the 'original male
person', usually translated into English as 'spirit'. The
meaning and usage of the word 'spirit' in English is wide and
various, and usually vague enough to sustain both definite
and very indefinite interpretations. In the context of this
verse its nearest equivalent in historical English usage is
'soul', which carries the meaning, however uncertainly, of
some sort of imperishable representation of our inmost self.
Just as undeveloped matter is described as having neither
beginning nor end and is therefore itself imperishable – the
perishable being only its developed forms – so the 'soul' is
imperishable in the perishable human shape in which it is
embodied. In this philosophy the mind is material, and the
ego-self is a product of material nature. It is only *purusha*
that stands above matter, mind and the ego with its passions,
desires, attachments and ambitions. This 'spirit' or 'soul' is
the witness of the antics of the material dressed in the motley
form of the ego-self. It is the true self, the subjective self,
the supreme or highest self, the supreme *atman* and, in the
context of this chapter, the 'knower of the field'.

While, in the *samkhya* system, *purusha* can be
described as immortal and pre-existing, as though pervasive
in the external universe, and in this way provide a rational
explanation of how it turns up 'undivided' (13:16) in each

material being, in effect, and in direct experience, it is the 'endlessness within' (2:17) of the self proper. For this reason I have not introduced either 'spirit' or 'soul' to stand for *'purusha'*, but designated it here as the 'immaterial' in contrast with the 'material' (*prakriti*) that it complements. It is only ever embodied as the 'self', the non-acting self standing above the actions of the ego-self that, as we learn here, are prompted by the *gunas* and belong to the organism's material nature. *Purusha* is not, and should not be mistaken for, agency, which is the province of the material (13:20).

moods and motions. 'changeability' (of the field, of mind-body).

temperaments. '*gunas*'.

13:21
for good or ill. 'in good or evil wombs'.

13:23
in whatever state of being. At whatever stage in the endless cycle of rebirth he has reached ('for good or ill', as in 13:21) he is released from that cycle by the realisation of the highest self as 'witness, permitter, supporter, experiencer', free from attachment to the actions of the *gunas* that belong to his material, mental, emotional nature.

13:24
the discipline of knowledge. 'the yoga of samkhya', carrying the same meaning as *jnana-yoga*.

the discipline of action. '*karma-yoga*'.

13:25
This is a definitive statement that it is sufficient for the

layman to pass beyond the cycle of rebirth by turning towards the truth of these teachings and away from his material attachments in an act of self-devotion. To be devoted to the highest concept of oneself, to look down from a higher vantage point upon one's material obsessions and the passions and emotions which arise from those material concerns, is already to be free of the rule of the *gunas*, and the 'moods and motions' of the 'field' which have bound the individual to the endless repetition of the same errors of ignorance.

13:26
union. That is, the union of the material with the immaterial, *prakriti* with *purusha*, what is to be known with that which knows.

13:27
the supreme ruler. 'the supreme lord', the self.

the everlasting in the transient form. 'the imperishable in the perishable'.

13:28
he cannot harm the self. 'he does not harm the self by the self'. It would be easy to interpret this verse, as both Edgerton and Sargeant do, as meaning that, since the supreme self is the same in all beings, realising this we should wish to refrain from harming anyone. However, it is clear from the following verse that what is meant here is that the self does not act and is beyond harm (2:23), that the actions of the ego-self are performed by material nature at the instigation of the *gunas*. The point is the same as that made in Book 2 at the scene of the battle: that the forms of the self perish but the supreme self cannot be killed or harmed, either in oneself or one's enemies (see 2:17 *et seq.*). The sense of the

verse is far removed from a pacifist manifesto.

13:30
that supreme state. 'brahman'. He who realises the supreme
state of selfhood is the witness and observer of the modes
of his material being, and sees himself not as the doer but as
the experiencer.

13:33
the owner of the field. Subjective consciousness, the self, the
'knower of the field' illumines the 'field' as the object.

14

HE WHO SITS APART

To be in any form, what is that?
(Round and round we go, all of us, and ever come back thither)
Walt Whitman, *Song of Myself*

14:1   I shall speak once more of wisdom,
      that highest wisdom
      all wise men have known,
      who, knowing it, have gone from here
      and have ascended to supreme perfection.
14:2   Those who by this wisdom
      have become at one with me
      were never born, unborn
      even from creation.
      Neither do they fear the end of all.

14:3   Great *brahman* is my womb
      and I the seed
      from which all beings arise.
14:4   Whatever forms they take
      from any womb
      great *brahman* is the womb
      and I the father and the seed.

14:5   The *gunas* of one's nature,
      which is born of matter –
      sattva, rajas, tamas –
      bind the self within the body.
14:6   *Sattva*, meaning purity
      and health and light,

binds it by attachment
to happiness and knowledge.

14:7   *Rajas*, meaning passion,
born of desire,
binds it by attachment
to the world of action.

14:8   *Tamas*, being dark,
is born of ignorance.
It leads the self astray
and binds it to delusion,
indolence and sleep.

14:9   Attachment to our happiness
is caused by *sattva*.
Rajas is the cause of our attachment
to our actions.
Tamas obscures wisdom
and is the cause of our attachment
to delusions.

14:10   *Sattva* arises when it dominates
rajas and *tamas*.
Likewise *rajas* may prevail
or *tamas* dominate.

14:11   When at every gate
the body bears the light of wisdom,
know that *sattva* has prevailed.

14:12   Greed, ambition, the restless
need to act,
arise when *rajas* dominates.

14:13   Dullness, lethargy,
neglectfulness, delusion,
mean that *tamas* has arisen
and prevailed.

14:14   At the time of death,
when *sattva* is predominant,

the self within the body
joins the stainless world
of those who know the highest.

14:15 He who dies
with *rajas* dominant
is born again an active man,
and he with *tamas* in ascendancy
is born once more a fool.

14:16 We say that actions
are properly performed
when purely *sattvic*.
But only suffering can come from *rajas*,
and ignorance from *tamas*.

14:17 Wisdom is born of *sattva*,
desire of *rajas*,
delusion, ignorance, neglectfulness
from *tamas*.

14:18 The *sattvic* will rise up,
the *tamasic* will go down,
and those who are *rajasic*
will remain midway between.

14:19 He who sees
no other doer
but the *gunas*,
who knows
that which is higher
than the *gunas*,
such a one attains
my state of being.

14:20 When the self transcends the *gunas*
that arise in its material body,
it is released from birth and death,
old age and suffering,
and finds its true immortal state.

14:21   What then is the character
of one who has transcended these three *gunas*?
How does he behave,
how does he transcend them?

14:22   He neither craves nor shuns
the presence or the absence
of insightfulness, of busyness
or of delusion.

14:23   He who sits apart
as though indifferent,
and undisturbed by any of the *gunas*,
thinking: It is the will at work,
and holds his ground and does not falter,

14:24   self-contained and constant,
for whom both pain and pleasure are alike,
to whom a stone, a clod of earth,
or gold are all the same,
holding all things equal:
likes and dislikes,
praise or blame,

14:25   esteem, dishonour,
friend or enemy
(not taking either part),
renouncing every call to act –
this man, we say,
transcends his temperament.

14:26   And one who serves me
with unwavering devotion,
who in this way transcends
the *gunas*, prepares himself
for union with *brahman*.

14:27   For I am the foundation,

the fount of the immortal and eternal,
the source of everlasting truth,
the absolute of bliss.

NOTES ON THE TEXT AND TRANSLATION

Book 14 is largely a more detailed treatment of the *samkhya* theory of the *gunas* which give rise to the various temperaments, characters and actions of created beings. We have already encountered the *gunas* (see Notes to 2:45 and 7:12) which in the text I have translated as 'temperaments' and sometimes as 'passions'. They are, as we have noted, literally 'strands' that make up the characteristic tempers or 'humours' of the personality in which one may be more dominant than the others. ('Temperament' is defined in mediaeval philosophy as a combination in proportion of elements or qualities that determine the material character of any body, animate or inanimate, so the concept of the *gunas* is by no means alien to our Western heritage of pre-scientific currents of thought. In English usage 'temperament' has replaced 'temper' in its former sense: 'What is temper?' asked George Eliot. 'Its primary meaning, the proportion and mode in which qualities are mingled, is much neglected in popular speech...'[1]). The three *gunas* of *sattva*, *rajas* and *tamas* do not translate any more readily than '*gunas*', and as this is a technical treatise designed to give a theoretical interpretation of the material nature of the will acting in the body and shaping the character and behaviour of the individual, I have retained Sanskrit terminology throughout this chapter except where the structure and meaning of the verse permit some flexibility.

14:1
I shall speak. 'I shall declare' or explain, but in fact he simply asserts it in this verse and 14:2.

---

[1] Eliot, George. *Only Temper* in *Impressions of Theophrastus Such*. London: William Pickering, 1994. (1879).

14:3
This verse and its coupling are disconnected from the two preceding verses and seem to be inserted here to elaborate the theme of 'creation' in 14:2. In the *samkhya* system, the primal seeding of creation is represented by the union of *purusha* with *prakriti*, the creative spirit with primal matter, the 'uncreated' self with the forms of being that return with each successive birth, and with each cycle of creation.

14:5
If the section that begins here is connected to the previous verses it is only by the loose association of the 'forms' arising from various 'wombs' with that which is the originator of the three *gunas*: 'All three states of being come from me.' (7:12).

14:6
It may seem strange that *sattva*, which represents the intelligent, moral, balanced and healthy-minded 'good' temperament, attached to the goals of happiness and understanding, should be treated on equal footing with *rajas* and *tamas* as a strand of one's material nature that binds the imperishable self to its body. We shall learn later that the predominance of the *sattvic* state is prerequisite for securing rebirth via the path of 'light' in contrast to the 'dark' path. But rebirth – for better of for worse – is the fate of everyone's material nature. Only the realised self is not reborn. So *sattva* is just as binding, despite its being the preferred state or attitude of an embodied being, for seeing happiness in anything other than release, and knowledge in anything other than the wisdom of the self, only serves to guarantee one's eternal recurrence. Since *sattva* is associated with 'goodness', this is a particular difficulty for those interpreters of the *Gita* who fail to grasp the role of the non-acting self and the absence of agency in the unfolding of its actions, and who reduce the ideal of *the absence of the self in action*

to 'selflessness' or 'unselfishness' in (good) 'works', which in reality is nothing more than the *sattvic guna* at work, attaching the self to a narrative of the 'good' person, a narrative the self must transcend if it is to realise its eternal, unchanging and inviolable 'highest state'.

14:11
The meaning is that wisdom dominates the influence of the senses that are the 'gates' of the body (see 5:13) and shines out of it.

14:14
The self, however, remains attached to *sattva*. Only by transcending all three characteristics of its bodily state, governed by the actions of its material nature, does the self find release from the wheel of birth and death and reach 'immortality' (14:20). This verse, along with 14:15, appears to refer to the 'light' and 'dark' paths, or the 'upper', 'middle' or 'lower' ways (14:18) to good or bad 'wombs' of rebirth (see 6:40 *et seq.* and 8:23 *et seq.*). The 'highest' referred to at the close of this verse is the 'upward' path.

14:15
an active man. 'as one attached to action'.

14:16
when purely sattvic. That is, when performed with the right motives.

14:18
These are the three transmigratory routes leading to lower or higher conditions of rebirth. *All* are reborn.

14:19
that which is higher. The supreme self that stands above the

gunas, above the actions of the will, that is also cognate with the 'me' or 'my state of being' in the *Gita*. It is not the same 'highest' referred to in 14:14. The self is beyond birth and death.

14:21
The question introduces a further description of the qualities of the one who renounces attachment to the promptings of his natural will, and the verses that follow echo passages from earlier sections.

14:22
That is, he is indifferent to each and all of the three *gunas*.

14:24
to whom a stone etc. This passage is taken from 6:8.

14:25
his temperament. 'the *gunas*' that make up his entire will to act in a particular characteristic way, recognising that 'it is the will at work' and not the self that is the agent.

14:26
In this coda the devotee is also included, in keeping with earlier sentiments that devotion, the turning away from the binding power of the material will towards the source of release, will at least go some way towards the ultimate goal.

14:27
For I am the foundation. 'For I am the foundation of *brahman*'. The '*brahman*' of the opening verses is reintroduced at 14:26. In 14:27 the self is assigned its fundamental founding role as that which supports the impersonal sustaining principle of creation, for ultimately *brahman* must be subject to the self which contains all, which is the seed of all.

15

BUT THERE IS SOMETHING OTHER

They are but parts, any thing is but a part.
Walt Whitman, *Song of Myself*

15:1   They speak of the eternal tree,
       those with knowledge of the Vedas,
       the fig that has its roots above,
       its branches in the earth below,
       whose leaves are vedic hymns.

15:2   Above, below, its branches spread,
       nourished by the *gunas*,
       from which the objects of the senses
       grow like shoots,
       and sends its roots
       out in the world,
       engendering men's actions.

15:3   Its form here in the world,
       without beginning, without end,
       is not to be found, not to be known.
       To cut the fig tree
       from its well-established root
       with a strong blow
       of the axe of non-attachment

15:4   is to seek out that abode
       from which, when reached,
       no one need return:
       he takes his refuge
       in that first creative spirit
       from which all things have flowed.

15:5   Free from pride, delusion and desire,
       conquering the evils of attachment
       and those opposites called happiness and sorrow,
       living always in the supreme self,
       the undeluded reach that everlasting goal.

15:6   Unlit by sun or moon or fire,
       that place to which one goes
       and never comes again –
       that is my highest home.

15:7   I merely share myself
       with each eternal self
       that comes to be by drawing
       to itself the senses and the mind
       existing in material nature.

15:8   The lordly self
       takes on his mortal form,
       and leaves it,
       carrying them along
       as the wind takes up
       and carries
       perfumes from their source.

15:9   He holds dominion
       over all the senses:
       sight and hearing,
       touch and taste and smell,
       and, finally, the mind.
       Their realm is his to own.

15:10   Those who are deluded
       do not see him,
       whether he has gone
       or whether he is here

as owner of the senses
or the temperaments.
Only to the eye of wisdom
is he visible.

15:11 Only those who strive to see him,
following the discipline of wisdom,
see him in the self.
But those who never think
and lack the discipline,
though they may strive
they shall not see him.

15:12 Know the splendour of the sun
that lights the universe is mine,
the moonlight and the firelight are mine.

15:13 On earth I am the strength
of beings, the living fuse of plants,
and I become the very taste of soma.

15:14 I am the digestive fire
and the breath of beings
in whom I dwell,
united with the inhalation
and the exhalation of the vital
and abdominal breath,
digesting the four foods.

15:15 The hearts of all men have I entered,
bestowing knowledge, memory and reason.
I am all the scriptures teach,
their author and their teacher.

15:16 The world of being has two forms,
the perishable and the indestructible.
Beings are its perishable form,
the changeless its eternal nature.

15:17 But there is something other

that is higher, called the supreme self,
that takes possession of the world,
the lord who bears it up eternally.

15:18   Since I transcend the perishable
and I am that other that is higher
than the indestructible,
I am celebrated as the supreme spirit
in the world and in the Vedas.

15:19   The undeceived
who knows me as the supreme spirit
devotes himself to me with all his being.

15:20   Thus by this secret doctrine that I teach
a man may waken to enlightenment
and act according to his duty.

NOTES ON THE TEXT AND TRANSLATION

Book 15 is a rather fragmented chapter in which it is difficult to discover a consistent narrative. It begins with a confused analogy, originally applied to the Vedas, in which the roots and branches of the eternally renewed sacred fig bring to mind both the endless cycle of rebirth caused by the work of the *gunas*, and the unknowable and imperishable form of *brahman*. The first four verses are perhaps linked to what has gone before in Book 14 on the subject of the *gunas*. Taking its cue from 15:4, 15:5 veers off into a further description of the supreme self and its 'abode'. Subsequent verses (15:7 to 15:12) extol the lordly power of the supreme self over the material form of being, interrupted by an interpolation at 15:12 to 15:15. The chapter ends with a reassertion that 'this' is 'my secret doctrine', though little of a formal nature has been said that has not been more fully iterated elsewhere.

15:1

the eternal tree. 'the eternal *ashvattha* tree'. This is the 'sacred fig' whose branches are separately rooted in the ground. The tree is associated with and consecrated to Vishnu. The analogy is a brahmanic one, here adapted and developed, rather awkwardly, to symbolise eternal recurrence through attachment and the role of the *gunas* and the senses in engendering motivated action in the world.

15:3

There is a similar metaphor in 4:42. And a parallel in Dickens: 'Self; grasping, eager, narrow-ranging, over-reaching self; with its long train of suspicions, lusts, deceits, and all their growing consequences; was the root of the vile tree.'[1]

---

[1] Dickens, Charles. *Martin Chuzzlewit*

15:4
no one need return. See 8:16

15:6
See the parallel with 8:26 and preceding verses that relate to the light and dark pathways to rebirth. Prabhavananda and Isherwood gloss 'that place' as being 'self-luminous', its most likely import.

15:7
This is *purusha* descending into its material form by gathering to itself the five senses plus the mind (the sixth sense) from pre-existent matter. It would be wrong to interpret the opening lines to mean 'an individual (and eternal) self is merely a fragment of myself' since the self can never be divided. Rather, the self is the same eternal self in all beings, which is made clear once more in the next verse.

15:8
The lordly self. 'The lord'.

his mortal form. 'his body'.

carrying them along. The senses and the mind referred to in the previous verse.

from their source. That is, from their origin in material nature.

15:11
those...following the discipline of wisdom. 'yogins'. The import being that those who wish to see the eternal in the self must perfect themselves through the discipline of the *yoga* teaching. It is not enough to have the desire and then not follow the right path.

15:13

soma. The (formerly) intoxicating drink dedicated to the vedic gods. See 9:20 and Note.

15:14

the four foods. Foods that are chewed, swallowed, drunk or just tasted.

15:15

I am all the scriptures teach. The literal translation of this passage is: 'I alone am what is to be known in all the Vedas, the author of the Vedanta (the Upanishads) and the knower of the Vedas.'

15:16

The world of being has two forms. 'There are two *purushas* (spirits) in the world'. This verse should be read in conjunction with the verse that follows, which identifies the 'third' supreme spirit. It is only this insistence on the use, in 15:17, of the 'highest' *purusha* that is above both of the others that, I believe, has required '*purusha*' in this line as poetic licence for '*prakriti*' in actual meaning, as Hill also surmises. To translate the line literally as, 'There are two *spirits* in the world', would be misleading. The meaning is more: 'The nature of the world (of being, of existence) has a twofold condition.' Prabhavananda and Isherwood translate '*purusha*' as 'personality'.

15:17

But there is something other. 'The highest *purusha* is something other'.

the world. 'the three worlds'.

15:20

according to his duty. The point of this statement is to restore the central tenet of this 'secret doctrine', that the self is above actions and that all actions and obligations are matters of caste duty and not conscience.

16

THE THREEFOLD GATES OF DARKNESS

I am the poet of the Body and I am the poet of the Soul,
The pleasures of heaven are with me and the pains of hell are with me
Walt Whitman, *Song of Myself*

16:1   To be without fear and pure in heart,
        inwardly directed to the path of wisdom;
        to be charitable towards others;
        to act with self-restraint;
        to worship and to read the scriptures;
        to practise righteousness and self-denial,
16:2   renunciation, non-violence and truthfulness;
        to be without anger and at peace;
        not to disparage others
        but to act with compassion to all;
        gentle, modest, constant, free from lust;
16:3   possessed of dignity, courage and forbearance;
        clean in mind and body,
        without malice towards others
        or pride in himself:
        these are the marks of the man
        born to be divine.

16:4   Dishonest, arrogant, conceited,
        angry, vulgar, ignorant:
        such is the manner of the man
        born demonic.

16:5   The thinking is:
        the attributes that lead

to liberation are divine;
the demonic lead to bondage.
Have no fear,
for you are born
endowed with the divine.

16:6   Two kinds of beings
are there in this world,
one divine and one demonic.
So far I have spoken of the one at length,
now hear from me
the nature of the other, the demonic.

16:7   The demonic do not understand
when to act, when not to act.
They have no sense of decency,
behave badly,
and no truthfulness is found in them.

16:8   They say there is no ground of truth,
no God, no cause or reason in the world,
that all this comes about
through lust.

16:9   Those who hold this view
are lost souls
of small intelligence,
given to evil ways,
born enemies of the world
for its destruction.

16:10   Intoxicated by insatiable desire,
hypocritical and filled with self-esteem,
in this deluded state they've taken hold
of false ideas and impure motives.

16:11   Endless anxiety is their lot,
that only ends with death.
Fulfilment of desire
is all that they hold dear,
convinced that there is nothing else
but this.

16:12   Trapped by the snares of a hundred hopes,
and given to lust and anger,
they seek out wealth by any means
to satisfy their craving.

16:13   'This is what I've gained today,
this I wish to have tomorrow.
This wealth is mine
and this more will be mine.

16:14   'Such and such an enemy
I have killed, and others
also will I slay.
I am the lord, these are my pleasures,
I am successful, powerful and happy.

16:15   'I am rich and high-born.
There is no one else like me.
I pray, I give to charity,
I am entitled to enjoy myself.'
So say the ignorant and deluded.

16:16   Carried away by their fantasies,
caught in a net of illusions,
obsessed with satisfying their desires,
they fall into the foulest hell.

16:17   Self-centred and unbending,

with that arrogance and self-conceit
that comes with wealth,
they merely go through motions of devoutness
and do not follow moral precepts.

16:18   Harnessed to their egos,
to their personal power,
their arrogance, desires and anger,
these ill-thinking men
hate me
embodied in the self
and in the selves of others.

16:19   These are the worst of men,
cruel and hateful.
Time and time again
I hurl them back
into demonic births.

16:20   Even so, for those deluded souls
emerging time and time again
who never try to reach me,
something lower still awaits them:

16:21   the threefold gates of hell –
desire, greed and anger –
the three destroyers of the self
one must renounce.

16:22   A man who thus escapes
the threefold gates of darkness
does the best thing for the self
and makes his way
towards the highest goal.

16:23   He who follows only his desires

and casts aside
the moral teachings of the scriptures
will never find perfection, happiness,
nor that highest goal.

16:24 Take your standards from the scriptures.
Know what must be done
and what must not be done
and, knowing this, act in the world
according to your obligations.

NOTES ON THE TEXT AND TRANSLATION

Book 16 deals with the two contrasting conditions and dispositions of men, here identified as the 'divine' and the 'demonic'. They both arise from material nature and the strands of the *gunas*. Throughout the *Gita* the *yogin*, with his understanding of and adherence to the teaching, and his will to reach an enlightened state, has been opposed to the 'deluded' and the ignorant who never free themselves from their ego-driven worldly and material attachments. But here we have a much more severe condemnation of the demonic, not just for their arbitrarily evil and selfish qualities but for their enmity towards God, reason and the self within. Men are not merely to be categorised as 'good' or 'bad' in spite of themselves, but divided, eternally, between those who strive towards the divine and those who turn away from it and seek only power for themselves in a material existence that is destructive of the self. They are marked, in particular, by hypocrisy in their acts of devotion and piety.

16:2
non-violence. '*ahimsa*', 'non-harming'.

16:5
The thinking is. 'It is thought'. The verse is addressed to Arjuna, who has shown himself as one who has embraced the path of wisdom.

16:7
when to act. They are driven by their own interests, desires and passions and do not distinguish acts of duty (when to act) and the self that is above action. The demonic are attacked here not simply because they behave badly but because they have no understanding of the nature of action and non-action.

16:9

lost souls. 'lost selves'.

16:17

they merely go through motions. Referring to 16:15: 'I pray, I give to charity'.

16:21

the threefold gates of hell. Worse than being simply born again into the same demonic state is the prospect of destroying the self, the only realised condition of being worth striving for, by passing through the gates of hell (the attachment to desire, greed and anger), never able to turn back. This is, of course, figurative language. These are the would-be destroyers of the self. The self is indestructible, but in truth its relentless rejection, one's permanent blindness to it brought about by myopic greed and the gratification of the ego and its will to power ('there is nothing else but this'), constitutes in effect its destruction. One becomes an enemy of one's own self (see 6:5-6:7), which is the worst fate than can befall us.

16:24

The self is above action. When the embodied self acts it does so from a clearly defined sense of duty, guided by standards derived from moral texts. He does not follow his own will, for his will is a delusion binding him to the impulses of his material nature. This is the essential moral dichotomy implicit in this teaching: the supreme self and sustainer does not act, is not therefore the agent, does not therefore act with conscience; the embodied being should follow the *dharma* of duty and obligation determined for all beings in the absolute social and moral order of the caste system and the precepts of religion, which serve as the conscience of the whole world.

17

FAITH IS THE ESSENCE OF A MAN

...faithful of days and faithful of nights...
Walt Whitman, *Song of Myself*

17:1   Those who cast aside
the moral precepts,
yet worship full of faith,
how do they stand?
Are they *sattvic* or *rajasic* or *tamasic*?

17:2   A man's faith is of three kinds,
born of his innate nature:
sattva, rajas, tamas.
Now hear of this.

17:3   As a man's nature is,
so is his faith.
Faith is the essence of a man.
As his faith is,
so is he.

17:4   The *sattvic* natured worship the gods,
the *rajasic* imps and demons.
For the rest, *tamasic* men
worship ghosts and the spirits of the dead.

17:5   No rule of scripture has endorsed
the terrible austerities
that men inflict upon themselves

with violence and passion
through self-deceit and egotism,
17:6   torturing the aggregate of elements
that forms the body. In this way
mindlessly they torment me,
the self within the body.
Know they are demonic types.

17:7   But all men also have three kinds
of preferences for food,
just as their forms of worship,
austere practices and giving differ.
Now hear of this.

17:8   *Sattvic* personalities prefer a diet
that is healthy, promoting life
and wellbeing, strength, happiness
and fulfilment – foods that are flavoursome,
wholesome and easy to digest.
17:9   *Rajasic* people go for sharp and sour foods,
salty, over-spiced, harsh and fiery –
foods that burn, creating pain
and suffering and sickness.
17:10   The *tamasic* are content
with stale and tasteless food,
food gone bad, leftovers,
even unfit food.

17:11   Worship for its own sake
in observance of the scriptures,
bearing in one's mind this only thought:
It should be done –
that is *sattvic*.
17:12   But worship with some end in mind,
and ostentatious offerings,

are all *rajasic*.

17:13   Worship without faith,
disregarding text and sacred utterance,
offering neither food nor fee,
they see entirely as *tamasic*.

17:14   These are called austerities of the body:
the worship of the gods; respect
towards the twice-born, the teacher
and the man of wisdom;
cleanliness of mind and body;
virtue, continence, non-violence.

17:15   Austerities of speech are these:
words that do not cause offence;
truthful, pleasing, profitable speech;
the practice of reciting to oneself
the sacred texts.

17:16   Tranquillity, benevolence and silence,
self-restraint and purity of thought
are called austerities of mind.

17:17   These three austerities
when practised with the highest form
of faith by steadfast men
expecting no reward,
are seen as *sattvic*.

17:18   Hypocritical performance
for the sake of good opinion,
courting reverence and respect –
such austerities are said to be *rajasic*,
uncertain and ephemeral.

17:19   Self-tormentors with mistaken
notions of the self,
or seeking by self-harm
the power to harm others,
are said to be *tamasic*.

17:20   A gift given with no other thought
        than that it should be given,
        given to a worthy person
        to whom we owe no favour,
        and given at the proper time and place:
        that gift is known as *sattvic*.

17:21   But what is given with reluctance,
        and with some benefit in mind,
        is thought of as *rajasic*.

17:22   A gift given at an inappropriate time
        and place to one who is unworthy,
        or given without due respect
        or with contempt, is said to be *tamasic*.

17:23   The sacred invocation
        OM, *TAT*, *SAT*
        the Brahmins have ordained
        from ancient times
        to be the threefold formula
        for *brahman*, the Vedas and the rites.

17:24   Therefore, as prescribed for them,
        all ritual acts, austerities and acts of giving
        are begun with *OM*
        by these expounders and interpreters
        of *brahman*.

17:25   *TAT* is said by those who seek their liberation
        with no thought of a reward
        from acts of sacrifice, austerities
        or various forms of giving.

17:26   *SAT* means both the real and the good,
        used also for good actions.

17:27   Constancy in worship,
        giving and austerity and acts
        that serve these purposes
        are also good.

17:28   Offerings and austerities
         practised without faith
         are the opposite of good:
         there is nothing for us
         either in this world or in the next.

NOTES ON THE TEXT AND TRANSLATION

The question, given to Arjuna, that opens Book 17, takes its cue from 16:23 and introduces a discursion into the role of the *gunas* in forming the character of men's faith. In this view it is a man's innate character that determines his beliefs, his natural and instinctive inclination towards one sort or another of external dependency, ranging from worship of the gods (a *sattvic* temperament) to petitioning ghosts and spirits (a *tamasic* tendency). There then follows an attack on the practice of extreme austerities and self-mortification (17:5-17:6). After this anatomisation of contemporary practices, a 'but' introduces a discourse on *sattvic, rajasic* and *tamasic* dietary preferences and their relationship to personality types (a theory still very much in vogue), returning at 17:11 to the main themes of worship, giving and self-restraint ('austerities') in the man of faith.

It is to be remembered that in order to achieve self-realisation, and to act in accordance with duty, to 'know what must be done and what must not be done' (16:24), we are to transcend the *gunas* by detaching the subjective self from their actions as agents. *Sattva*, therefore, is also to be overcome, and since the worship of the gods (that is, the gods of the Aryan pantheon) arises from the influence of *sattva*, it follows that we must go beyond our attachment to those gods and any expectations we have of them as external influencers of our destiny. Despite the many colourations of the text, here and throughout the more 'orthodox' passages of the *Gita*, the contrast (developed explicitly in Book 7) between the *yoga* of self-detachment, which has self-realisation as the 'highest goal', and the material nature of other forms of dependent religious worship and sacrifice remains clear. Their conflicting positions is only resolved on the common ground of a selfless and detached attitude of mind towards all that may be regarded as superior to one's unworthy desires and thus worthy of veneration. The latter section of the chapter contrives a tentative reconciliation between the brahmanic religion and the *yogic* way.

17:3

Faith is a matter of nature and instinct. A man's innate character determines his faith; his faith makes his character. 'As men are, so are their gods,' wrote Amiel.[1]

17:6

demonic types. Those referred to in Book 16. See 16:18.

17:13

fee. Payment (or gift) to the priest.

they. Indicating we are here (and throughout the rest of the chapter) being referred again to a received body of doctrine on the nature and actions of the *gunas.*

17:14

austerities. The 'true' austerities of 17:14-17:16 are in contrast to the violent austerities described in 17:5-17:6. 'Austerity' is used within a fairly wide compass to mean the practice of self-restraint and self-discipline in thought, word and deed in one's attitude towards the spiritual life.

the twice-born. The common epithet for the Brahmin.

continence. The word in this context has a particular reference to vows of chastity.

non-violence. '*ahimsa*'.

---

[1] Amiel, Henri Frédéric. *The Private Journal of Henri Frédéric Amiel*, translated by Van Wyck Brooks and Charles Van Wyck Brooks. New York: Macmillan, 1935. (Journal entry for November 10, 1852).

17:18

uncertain. 'unsteady', contrasted with the 'steadfastness' of men who are grounded in their faith (17:17).

17:19

the power to harm others. All throughout the history of Hinduism the practice of extreme austerities, self-mortification and indulgence in a number of macabre practices, has been undertaken solely for the purpose of acquiring magical powers over others.

17:23

OM. See Note to 7:8. '*TAT*' and '*SAT*' are explained in the verses that follow.

17:25

TAT. 'THAT', 'that which is', the affirmation of *brahman*.

17:26

SAT means both the 'real' or the 'true' and the 'true' and the 'good'. That what *is*, (*TAT*) is 'good' (*SAT*), whether it is light or dark, is the primal universal affirmation of the real, common to such widely disparate sources as the Judaic creation myth and the songs of the pygmies of the Congo: 'And God saw the light, that it was good'[1] and 'If darkness is, it is good'[2].

17:27

'good'. 'SAT'.

17:28

the opposite of good. 'asat'.

---

[1] *Genesis* 1:4

[2] Pygmy song recorded by Colin Turnbull: Turnbull, Colin M. *The Forest People*. London: Jonathan Cape, 1961.

18

THE TRUE AND GOOD ABANDONER

All truths wait in all things,
They neither hasten their own delivery nor resist it
Walt Whitman, *Song of Myself*

18:1   I wish to know
       what it means
       to put aside
       and what it means
       to leave behind,
       and how they differ.

18:2   To put aside
       those actions prompted by desire
       is in the view of sages
       called renunciation.
       To put behind them
       things accruing from their actions
       is called abandonment
       by those who see this clearly.

18:3   Thus some philosophers have said
       that every form of action is an evil
       and ought to be abandoned.
       Others say that worship, giving
       and austerities are actions
       not to be abandoned.

18:4   Hear from me my own conclusions

on this matter of abandonment,
for three aspects are assigned to it.

18:5   Acts of worship, giving and austerities
are not to be abandoned
but should be done.
Worship, giving and austerities
sanctify the wise.

18:6   They must be done, however,
by first abandoning attachment to reward.
This is my ultimate conviction.

18:7   Indeed, renunciation of one's obligations
is not proper, and misguidedly
abandoning those actions
is judged to be *tamasic*.

18:8   On the other hand, abandonment of action
through fear of pain or bodily affliction
is *rajasic*, and nothing comes of it.

18:9   But, further, actions done
because they should be done,
without attachment to reward of any kind,
constitute the *sattvic* nature of abandonment.

18:10   Cut off from doubt, the learned man,
the true and good abandoner,
is not averse to actions that are inauspicious,
and nor is he attached to profitable actions.

18:11   Truly no one can abandon actions altogether.
One who gives up all he gains by actions
is called the true abandoner.

18:12   Threefold are the fruits of action
for non-abandoners
when they depart this life:
what they have wished for,

the undesired, or both;
but for renouncers of the fruits of action,
none at all.

18:13   Learn from me
the fivefold ground of action
that *samkhya* doctrine has propounded:

18:14   the body as the material cause;
the agent acting;
the instruments of action;
actions themselves;
and, fifthly, acts of providence.

18:15   In all man does or says or thinks,
for good or ill,
these five are the ground.

18:16   Since this is so,
one who sees the self alone as agent,
like a fool lacks understanding
and does not truly see.

18:17   One whose insight
has not been defiled
by this self-centred point of view,
when he acts to slay these people
does not slay them, is not bound.

18:18   Knowledge, its object and the knower –
these three are the impetus to action.
The instrument of action,
the act itself
and the agent acting
constitute the threefold ground of action.

18:19   The theory of the *gunas*
says that knowledge, action and the agent
are themselves divided into three,

determined by the *guna* strands.
Now hear of these.

18:20 Seeing in all beings
the one eternal being
undivided in the many:
know that this is *sattvic* knowledge.

18:21 But seeing each existence
as a separate entity,
differing in kind from one another,
is *rajasic* knowledge.

18:22 And holding on to one small thing
of no significance as though it were
the all of everything,
without a larger view of causes,
is said to be *tamasic*.

18:23 An action properly prescribed,
performed disinterestedly
and with detachment,
desiring nothing from it,
is known as *sattvic*.

18:24 Laboured actions
with some selfish end in mind,
are said to be *rajasic*.

18:25 Misguided actions,
with no thought of consequence
or loss or injury to others,
or those exceeding one's abilities,
are called *tamasic*.

18:26 One who acts
with freedom from attachment
and from self-regard,
resolute and firm,

impervious to success or failure,
is considered *sattvic*.

18:27 One who acts
from greed and passion,
seeking only to obtain what he desires,
violent, immoral, and subject to
the vagaries of happiness and grief,
is said to be *rajasic*.

18:28 One who acts
lacking self-control,
vain and stubborn,
deceitful and dishonest,
lazy, sullen and procrastinating,
is said to be *tamasic*.

18:29 Now hear from me in full
the threefold role the *gunas* play
in intellectual discrimination
and the firmness of the will.

18:30 To understand
when to act, when not to act,
which acts are right and which are wrong,
what is to be feared and what is not,
what binds us and what sets us free,
is *sattvic*.

18:31 The mind that can't distinguish
right from wrong,
duty from neglect of duty,
is *rajasic*.

18:32 The mind that in its blindness
takes wrong for right,
turning everything around perversely,
is *tamasic*.

18:33 The single-minded firmness
       of the will through *yoga*,
       the steady holding of the mind at bay,
       the breath, the senses:
       that is *sattvic*.
18:34 But clinging to the hope of gain,
       by holding on to status,
       wants and wishes and prosperity:
       that sort of firmness is *rajasic*.
18:35 That determination of a stupid man
       to never give up sleep
       or let go fear and grief,
       despondency and self-regard:
       that sort of firmness is *tamasic*.

18:36 Hear now from me
       how the happiness to be enjoyed
       from practice that brings
       suffering to an end
       is of three kinds.

18:37 That happiness is *sattvic*
       which arises from the clarity
       of one's own mind
       that from the beginning
       recognised as poisonous
       what in the end
       would be transformed to nectar.
18:38 Contentment with the sensual world
       that seems at first like nectar
       but turns to poison in the end
       is said to be *rajasic*.
18:39 That happiness that ends as it began
       in self-deception
       is said to be *tamasic*

and has its origins in sleepy-headed
laziness and apathy.

18:40   No being can exist,
        not here on earth
        and nor in heaven among the gods,
        free from these three influences
        arising from material nature.

18:41   How the Brahmins and *kshatriyas*,
        the *vaishyas* and the *shudras* act
        has been determined
        by the *gunas* of their innate natures.
18:42   How the Brahmin acts –
        tranquil of mind, austere and self-restrained,
        pure in mind and body, patient, upright,
        a man of wisdom, faith and understanding –
        is governed by his nature.
18:43   Heroic, princely,
        skilful and courageous,
        generous and noble,
        the *kshatriya* never flees the field.
        His sphere of action
        has been given by his nature.
18:44   Labour in the fields,
        herding cows and trading
        are what the *vaishya* does.
        The *shudra* serves.
        This has been determined
        by their natures.

18:45   A man content to do his own work
        finds fulfilment.
        Hear now how the man
        contented with his own work

finds fulfilment.

18:46 By his work he praises Him
from whom all things arise
and who is ever-present in the world.
In this he finds fulfilment.

18:47 Better your own duty,
though imperfect,
than another's duty well-performed.
Actions that arise
from one's own nature
incur no guilt.

18:48 No one should abandon
the work that he is born to do
in spite of faults,
for all beginnings
are obscured by error,
as fire is by smoke.

18:49 One whose mind is always unattached,
having conquered both the self
and its desires,
achieves that perfect state
of freedom from his actions
through renunciation.

18:50 Let me tell you briefly, then,
the way by which the one
who has achieved that perfect state
may also reach the highest state of knowledge,
which is to know the all-sustaining
power of the world.

18:51 He must be disciplined and pure of will
and firmly self-controlled,
abandoning the first and last
of all the objects of the senses,
dismissing passion and rejecting hate.

18:52   He sits alone, eats little,
         is moderate in speech,
         his mind and body under his control,
         constant in his practice of *yoga* meditation,
         dispassionate in his point of view.
18:53   One who has relinquished egotism,
         power, arrogance and desire,
         anger and possessiveness, and who
         is unacquisitive, at peace within,
         prepares himself to be at one
         with that one all-sustaining being.
18:54   At one with That,
         the self in its serenity
         with nothing to regret
         and nothing to be longed for,
         knowing all beings as the same,
         finds in me
         the highest object of devotion.

                    *

18:55   By devotion to Me
         does he come to know Me
         in my greatness as I truly am,
         and knowing Me in truth
         at once he comes to Me.
18:56   He who always acts in Me
         will through My grace
         attain to that eternal
         and immutable abode.
18:57   Keep Me always in your mind,
         surrender all your acts to Me,
         hold Me as the highest object,
         rely upon the will to understand.
18:58   Keep Me in your mind

and by My grace
you will surmount all hardships.
But if through vanity
you will not listen,
then you will be lost.

18:59 If, relying on yourself,
you think: I shall not fight,
in vain will you adhere to that resolve,
for mortal nature will compel you.

18:60 You are born to your own nature,
bound by your karma,
and even what you wish most not to do
in your deluded state of mind
you will do anyway, against your will.

18:61 The Lord dwells
at the heart of every being
and whirls them round
like a whirligig
by the magic of his power.

*

18:62 Go to Him with your whole being,
find in Him your refuge,
and by that grace
there also shalt thou find
supreme peace
and thine eternal resting place.

*

18:63 Thus have I taught you
knowledge more secret than secret.

Consider it in full
and do as you will.

18:64   Hear from Me again
My highest and most secret words:
I love thee well,
therefore shall I speak
to your advantage.

18:65   Devote your mind to Me,
worship Me, make sacrifice to Me,
bow down before Me,
then surely will you come to Me,
I promise, for thou art dear to Me.

18:66   Abandon all your duties,
trust in Me alone,
and I shall deliver you from evil.
Do not grieve.

*

18:67   This thou shalt not speak of
to any lacking in austerity,
nor to one who fails to worship,
nor at any time to those
who will not hear,
nor to those
who murmur against Me.

18:68   But whosoever teaches
to My worshippers
this supreme secret,
having shown supreme devotion to Me,
certainly shall come to Me.

18:69   In him, among all men,
am I well pleased,
None other is more dear to Me

on earth, nor shall be.

*

18:70 And he who shall recite
this sacred dialogue between us,
by him would I be worshipped
with the sacrifice of wisdom.
Thus do I believe.

18:71 He who hears
and does not scorn it,
but hears it filled with faith,
even he shall be released
into the splendid regions of the virtuous.

*

18:72 Have you heard this
with a concentrated mind,
O Arjuna,
and has your ignorance
and confusion passed?

18:73 O Krishna,
by your grace
doubt and confusion are dispelled.
I have come to myself.
I will carry out your word.

*

18:74 Sanjaya spoke:
Thus have I heard,
with hair erect,

the marvellous conversation
that took place 'twixt Krishna
and the great-souled Arjuna.

18:75   I, by Vyasa's grace,
have heard the supreme secret *yoga*
given by the Lord Himself,
Krishna, Lord of Yoga.

18:76   O King, remembering and remembering
this marvellous and sacred conversation
'twixt Krishna of the Handsome Hair
and Arjuna, over and over again
do I rejoice.

18:77   O King, remembering and remembering
the more than marvellous form
of Hari Krishna,
so great is my amazement
that over and over again
do I rejoice.

18:78   Where there is Krishna, Lord of Yoga,
where Arjuna the archer,
forever also will there be
glory, victory, wealth and prudent counsel.
Of this I have no doubt.

NOTES ON THE TEXT AND TRANSLATION

The question which opens the final chapter of the *Gita* introduces a distinction between the 'renunciation' (*sannyasa*) of motives attached to actions and the 'relinquishing' (*tyaga*) or abandonment of attachment to their results – that is, the renunciation of attachment to desires themselves and the subsequent attachment to the objects of desire, of both action and the fruits of action. These two forms of renunciation are defined in 18:2, and subsequent verses go on to note some conclusions in the debate about what sort of actions may be permitted, noting in particular acts of worship or sacrifice. A theory that eschews all motivated actions (including moral actions) and all the fruits of action inevitably leads to some uncertainty and controversy around what may be permitted in practical life, since, as the *Gita* itself points out, we *must* act. The problem is similar to that created by the Stoics in renouncing actions that are not purely virtuous or in accord with duty, but none the less could be considered conducive to virtue: for example, that the desire for health or freedom from pain might be considered legitimate goals in the pursuit of virtue and should be included as a 'good'.[1]

The bulk of the chapter is a roundup of some remaining points relating to action and duty, the role of the *gunas* and the position of the detached self in relation to the performance of actions in the world. It deals consecutively with the *gunas* of knowledge itself, describing the different qualities of knowledge in 18:20-18:22. The next three verses cover the qualities of 'action', and the following three (18:26-18:28) the qualities that adhere to the 'doer' or agent. The next sections, again in triads, differentiate acts of discrimination (*'buddhi'*) and firmness of will, finally

[1] See: Zeller, E. *Chapter 11* of *The Stoics, Epicureans and Sceptics*. London: Longmans, Green, and Co., 1892.

separating the nature of true contentment from the illusion of happiness.

The uncomfortable conclusion is that these qualities are all givens, and that both a man's disposition and his destiny are determined by material limitations. His character is determined by the innate nature of his material will (the *gunas*), through whose agency the condition into which he is born has also been determined. Neither can be changed, but both can be transcended.

Verse 18:54 marks the climax and the natural end of this sequence. Although this chapter is very much given over to the theory of the *gunas* and the destined duties of material beings in a material world, it follows through to its conclusion the central teaching given in the *Gita*: the self does not act; its only free actions are acts of devotion to a higher principle; actions are the domain of the material will manifest in the character and destiny of the individual; the discriminating will (*buddhi*) can determine to release the deathless self through renunciation, self-discipline and the practice of *yoga* – and by understanding the basic tenets of *samkhya* philosophy; by following this route the self (*atman*) is freed from the cycle of birth and death that belongs to its material nature and united with the impersonal sustaining principle of the world (*brahman*) in subjective consciousness as 'me', the realised state of transcendent and immortal being that is the 'highest object of devotion'.

There is, however, a significant coda to the entire *Gita*, beginning at 18:55 with a subtle and then more violent shift of focus from the 'me' that is the self to the 'Me' as the godhead and source of divine grace. What follows is an unsettled and unhappy amalgam of genuine *samkhya* doctrine, Vaishnava coloured reflections of earlier verses, *bhakti* cult intrusions and conclusions, and brahmanic usurpations as the text is stitched back into the Mahabharata story, culminating with its final and most disappointing lines.

18:1
to put aside. 'to renounce'.

to leave behind. 'to abandon'.

18:2
Despite this fine distinction between similar terms, subsequent verses use both indiscriminately. In translation I have followed the Sanskrit terms as they occur.

18:10
Cut off from doubt. See 4:41-4:42.

inauspicious. 'disagreeable' would be an alternative translation, but given a cultural preoccupation with auspicious and inauspicious times for action, 'inauspicious' seems appropriate to describe actions that are to be performed disinterestedly.

18:12
the fruits of action. It becomes clearer in this verse what is meant by the 'fruits' of action (which I have translated variously as 'gains', 'rewards' or 'things accruing', as well as the more literal 'fruits') and where attachment to them is leading. All actions, intentional and unintentional, have consequences. To act in order to gain something, and to feel either satisfaction or dissatisfaction with the results, is to bind oneself to the wheel of life and death, to eternal recurrence and to material being. Our only freedom lies in renunciation, not of action itself, which cannot be avoided, but of the fruits of action, the desire for which enslaves all beings to the eternal round of more of the same. In the *Gita* the word 'action' (*karma*) has three distinct usages, though they are often interrelated and can cause some confusion when they occur in close proximity. The first conveys

action in the world, exemplified by action in battle in the early part of the *Gita*, where the self is to be detached from the illusion of the self-as-agent in actions, and actions are to be performed as matters of duty. That is the context of verses 18:7-18:9. Secondly, the *yoga* discipline of action (*karma-yoga*) is distinguished from the *yoga* of knowledge (*jnana-yoga*) in arguing against withdrawal from the world in order to avoid the consequences of action by not acting. This difference between the two *yoga* schools is recollected in 18:3: 'some philosophers have said that every form of action is an evil'. The third usage carries the meaning of 'ritual action' where acts of sacrifice, worship, offerings and the undertaking of various degrees of austere or self-disciplined practices are designed to reap some benefit or reward, rather than being performed because they have value in themselves and sanctify the pure in heart (18:5-18:6). In all three instances, the renunciation of actions motivated by the desire for the ends or aims or fruits of action and the abandonment of attachments to the outcomes are necessary to free the self from its chains and liberate it from the eternal round, evoked in the merry-go-round image of verse 18:61. 18:12 says you get what you wish for, or you get what you least wanted (though perhaps the meaning is you avoid the unwished for), or you get a little of both when returned to earth. It makes no difference. You are destined to come back and do it all over again unless you find the way to step off the roundabout once and for all.

18:14
the instruments of action. The sensory and functional apparatus of the organism by which actions are accomplished.

18:17
does not slay them. That is, he does not slay them by the actions of the self as agent, which is an illusion; he himself is not the

cause. The verse recalls 2:19 and the scene of the battle.

18:18
Knowledge, its object and the knower. This statement reprises the passages in Book 13 dealing with the field and the knower of the field. The remainder of the verse brings into play three of the five grounds of action identified in 18:14 (the other two, the body itself as the material ground and fortuitous acts of providence, are not directly functional).

18:19
divided into three. The verses that follow apply the three *gunas* to these three elements: knowledge itself, the performance of actions and the temperament of the agent or doer. These numeric divisions and subdivisions remind us that '*samkhya*' can be translated as the 'enumerative' philosophy, attempting to bring some hierarchical rigour to all these elements.

18:20
This verse may be read in conjunction with 13:12-13:17 which describe the ultimate goal of knowledge.

18:30
the threefold role. The following three verses address the influence of the *gunas* of a man's character on his ability to make intelligent judgments. That discriminating intellect, or mind, is '*buddhi*' (see Note to 2:39). The next three (18:33-18:35) then characterise firmness of will and determination in men of different judgment.

18:32
in its blindness. 'enveloped in darkness'.

18:34
the hope of gain. 'the fruits of action'.

status. '*dharma*', meaning one's (given) rightful duty, in this instance as a measure of one's worth. We could summarise the meaning of this verse as 'concentrating only on being successful'.

18:36
practice. Since there are three qualities attached to intellectual discrimination and to willed determination, the qualities of 'happiness' (in this case contentment or satisfaction) will vary accordingly. *Sattvic* practice conforms with *yoga* discipline, whose pre-requirements are correct understanding (18:20), correct discernment (18:30) and correct discipline (18:33). Only this 'practice' can lead to 'happiness', which is freedom from suffering arising from attachment. The *rajasic* pursue happiness through success (18:34) that turns poisonous in the end. The *tamasic* simply remain in their deluded state from birth to death.

18:37
mind. '*atma-buddhi*', the discriminating self.

poisonous. It is attachment to the world of the senses and the pursuit of the fruits of action that have been recognised from the beginning as poisonous by the discriminating *sattvic* mind, which aims to conquer them. Though they seem sweet at first to the *rajasic* mind, only disillusion (poison) can follow.

18:40
influences. 'the *gunas*'. The transitional status of beings in heaven prior to rebirth is also determined by the *gunas*. There is no escape from the fatefulness of one's condition, which is the subject of the verses that follow.

18:41

These are the four main castes of the social order, determined by birth: the Brahmin (priestly) caste; the *kshatriya* warrior or princely caste to which Arjuna and Krishna belong; the *vaishya*, merchants, traders, farmers, peasants, labourers; the *shudra*, the servant classes. There are endless fine subdivisions of the latter two castes related to occupations. The section beginning with this verse describes the 'actions' (*karma*) of the castes, and not the 'duties' (*dharma*), which would be an incorrect translation. The actions of the Brahmin and the *kshatriya* in the verses that follow are described as innate qualities, but the actions of the *vaishya* and *shudra* are lumped together simply as activities.

18:46

Him, or 'That', meaning *brahman*, the all-embracing principle of order.

18:47

duty. '*dharma*'. This verse is a reworking of 3:35. Actions arising from one's material nature are the work of the *gunas*, and not the self. Evils arise only when we wilfully disrupt the natural order determined by birth.

18:49

This verse does not follow seamlessly from the preceding verse. However, the whole tendency of the chapter has been to reach this point of renunciation by first firmly associating all actions and works with the *gunas* of material nature and containing all *moral* actions within the limits of one's innate moral nature set by the *gunas* and denoted by birth. The way forward *now*, conclusively restating the doctrine given in Book 2 that was taken up again variously in 5:13-5:14 and 13:19-13:20, is to release the self from the illusion of agency (and thereby from guilt and moral culpability) by renouncing action and hence to realise the self in and *as* the eternal all-sustaining principle of being.

18:50
the all-sustaining power of the world. '*brahman*'.

18:51
abandoning the first and last. Literally, 'abandoning the objects of the senses, the first of which is sound'.

18:53
that one all-sustaining being. '*brahman*', referred to in 18:50.

18:54
finds in me the highest object of devotion. 'attains supreme devotion to me'.

18:56
grace. The concept of 'grace', which appeared in the Vaishnavite Book 11, is reintroduced. Although the underlying doctrine of self-realisation through the *yoga* of discrimination (see next verse) remains present, the 'me' here has become a divine agent, and it is through divine 'grace' that entry is granted to the 'eternal abode' which is both the goal of *yoga* discipline and the supreme object of devotion previously identified.

18:57
the will to understand. '*buddhi-yoga*', 'the discipline of willed discrimination'. This verse is a variant of 12:6.

18:58
vanity. 'egotism'.

18:59
yourself. 'your ego-self'.

mortal nature. '*prakriti*', 'material nature'.

18:60
karma. 'Karma' is left untranslated since it is used here, uniquely, in the sense in which it has been adopted into the language, from Buddhism, as 'fate' or 'destiny' determined by prior actions (*karma*). This represents a new determinist interpretation of *karma* and the theory of the *gunas* of material nature, closer in meaning to 'the will of God' (see next verse).

18:62
Go to Him. With this sudden, momentary shift to the third person, Krishna is no longer the speaker but the subject of this interpolated doctrinal verse, with its echoes of Christian devotional sentiments.

18:63
The doctrine is now declared to be a secret doctrine, the full knowledge of which entitles the recipient to act as he wills (which, of course, directly contradicts the determinist theory of action stated in 18:60). The import, however, is that Arjuna is now entitled, having been granted access to revealed secret knowledge by the grace of God, to act with impunity.

18:66
Abandon all your duties. This commandment is contrary to all that we have heard about following one's own *dharma*, without which the whole world falls into disorder and succumbs to evil. Many commentators have been at pains to recast this line to mean 'abandon all the fruits of actions',

but the statement is quite explicit, recalling the command of Jesus to his fishermen disciples to abandon their nets and 'follow me'. The similarities continue in 18:67-18:69.

18:70
the sacrifice of wisdom. For the meaning of 'the sacrifice of wisdom' see 4:33 and 9:15.

We are now standing outside the 'action' of the *Gita* looking at the established historical text itself, how it should be taught, who may teach it and who may hear it.

18:73
I have come to myself. 'I have gained recollection', that is, he has recovered his senses lost in 2:7-2:8. He now consents to follow the teaching of his master.

18:75
by Vyasa's grace. See references in 10:13 and 10:37 where Vyasa, as the author of the text, is referred to in a similar vein, and to which this verse relates.

Lord of Yoga. This title was given to Krishna in 11:19.

18:78
Having appropriated the 'secret' doctrine of *yoga* as the divine gift of Krishna, and consolidated the *Gita* text as the work of the author of the Vedas, the Brahmin has the last word, reclaiming the authority of the *Gita*, not as the way of liberation through renunciation, but as wise counsel on the field of battle that will assure victory and the assumption of power and wealth as the fruits of sanctified actions, to all of which the core teaching has been vehemently opposed. This is a remarkable reversal of fortune for the *Gita* at the point at which it is reintegrated into the great Aryan epic. It leaves

those who are not persuaded by this conclusion to go back and read this 'sacred dialogue' again and again, penetrating its multiple accretions, until the miasma of delusion and illusion, mysticism and mystification, is dispelled and the temptations of the material impulses of one's natural understanding are finally overcome. It requires patience.

All truths wait in all things,
They neither hasten their own delivery nor resist it

ACTION, NON-ACTION AND DEVOTION

If the *Iliad* deserves the title, *The Anger of Achilles*, bestowed on it by Robert Graves in his version of the Greek epic, the *Bhagavad Gita* might equally qualify to be called *The Guilt of Arjuna*. The uncompromising anger of Achilles at the injustice of his reward from the division of the spoils of war is the primary cause of the death and destruction that follows. Arjuna's sudden realisation that the conflicting claims to the prize of power and wealth of the two armies arrayed on either side of him will lead him to destroy his own kinsmen and bring guilt upon himself and evil upon his own clan, is the personal and temperamental situation from which this long interlude in the epic *Mahabharata* springs. That sense of guilt is at first formulated as the question: Why should I fight? But in the development of an answer, that question, by exploring the causes of action, the responsibilities imposed by duty, the role of the self as the agent of action, and the wilfulness of material nature itself, becomes a much broader and more complex one: In what circumstances can a man be said freely to act morally, and under what conditions are his actions free from guilt? The question: How should we act? is the question that every philosophy that is not solely speculative, and every religion, seeks to answer. This theme of action, of who or what acts, of the origin of the motives and impulses to act, of guilt and freedom from guilt, is the theme around which the many strands and the polyphony of voices in the *Gita* weave and harmonise and compete.

An inquiry which sets out to determine how we should live our lives naturally begins with what it understands of the material or 'objective' world in which we have our being, and of the 'subjective' faculty of the understanding itself that we believe gives us the right to make statements about either. We begin with ourselves, with our own experience, knowledge and understanding, because there is nowhere else to begin. Yet our experience is limited, our knowledge incomplete, our understanding imperfect and subject to revision. Any idea we form of the nature of the world and of ourselves is open to doubt: our memory does not extend to the whole of human experience; what we know does not represent all that can be known; our understanding is confined to those few things encountered in personal experience and through the accumulation of a little useful knowledge. But despite the undeniable uncertainty of our conception of the nature of the world and ourselves, we do not deny existence itself, nor the fact of existence as a personal subjective experience. There is nothing we can say, or think, or believe about anything at all that does not implicitly accept as its premise the objective existence of the world and its representation, in one form or another, in subjective experience.

This may all seem very obvious, but it is important to keep in mind, as we trace the sometimes disconnected threads of the argument in the *Gita*, the distinction between the purely objective world which has its own ground of being unrelated to us, and the world as it appears to us and about which we are always anxious to establish the 'truth'. We are in the habit of constantly ascribing to the objective world qualities that are purely the product of mental processes, processes which represent the world of appearances as something coherent, connected, distinct and real rather than as a confused tangle of sense impressions, a world as it might appear through a broken kaleidoscope. The world does not contain its own language, or reason, or symbols, its own explanation or justification, its own good or ill will, its own measure of itself. Every quality ascribed to it is assigned by our conscious faculty for perception and representation, by our capacity for language, symbolism, mathematics, description, measurement and definitive statement. The world, of course, exists as *something*. But what that something is in itself it is unable to declare, for all statements about it are necessarily made by the subject and are not the properties of the object itself. We can therefore distinguish a world of objective being, an impersonal world that does not disclose itself, from a personal world that is real to us in all its many dimensions, uniquely available in subjective experience.

From what we know of the universe and its evolutionary history, and from all that we have previously guessed at, it clearly has the inherent power to sustain itself and to produce and reproduce all material phenomena, from rocks and seas and clouds and volcanoes to slime moulds, trees, flowers, birds, beasts and human beings. That all-pervasive something from which everything else arises and into which it is dissolved but which itself is neither created nor destroyed, that is, the 'ground' of the universe as distinct from each and all of its material manifestations, is known, in the cosmological and cosmogonic context of the *Gita*, as *brahman*. It is creative and enduring, but also violent and destructive.

Brahman is not an intelligence, still less an intelligent 'agent' acting in and upon the universe. It is simply the sufficiency of the world to be the source of both material nature and the intelligence manifest in it. The world that existed before organic life appeared – the world of fire and water, earth and air and space, of sand and clay, sun and wind and rain – was without intelligence, contained no knowledge of itself, was without awareness of its existence or of the multiplicity of its temporal forms that came and went over aeons of time. The emergence of intelligence to explain it does not alter its fundamental nature. Intelligence, knowledge, and the formal representation in consciousness of the unconscious forms of the world and the already-created forms of ourselves do not in any degree affect the innate capacity of the world itself to stand, as it were, upon its own feet without justification. Nor does it change the fact that the objective matter of the world and the subjective matter of the intelligence are both the product and properties of the unmanifest and, in itself, unknowable and entirely impersonal and indifferent ground or principle upon which everything is founded:

> *Out of the unmanifest*
> *comes the manifest,*
> *the visible day,*
> *dissolving again*
> *into invisible night.* (8:18)

And yet, without the intelligence nothing really exists at all. We *say* the world 'out there' exists, and we say that we *know* the world existed before we were born and that it will continue without us, but saying and knowing both belong to a conscious intelligence manifest in the world that in itself is unmanifest. We only know what we know, as representation and appearance, as memory, as agreed upon facts in the history of experience. We do not know what it is like to not know, to be unknowable, to be an objective element of the universe. We only know what it is like to be the subject that knows, and the subject that thinks its knowledge of the world is the same as the world itself. We can say that the material world exists first, as a prior necessity, in which intelligence manifests itself. But we can equally say that intelligence *must* exist first before the world can be manifest to it, for where else can we look for the world but in our own knowledge of being in the world? We know nothing of the beginning of being and nothing of the end of being. We come out of and return to the unknowable, the unmanifest. We know about birth and death only as objective phenomena in the material world of which we have knowledge, as objects of knowledge and not as subjects of experience. The world exists *only* as knowledge, as subjective experience, and exists *always* as subjective experience because it cannot exist in any other manifest form. It can only otherwise be said to exist as an unmanifest principle. The fact is that the world that lies outside us and the world that rests within us, the world that is seen and known and the self that sees and knows it, are co-extensive. We can never say that one exists without simultaneously admitting the existence of the other.

With our modern scientific world-outlook we ought by now to have succeeded in redefining consciousness as 'nothing but' a sort of ghostly suspension of neurological impulses in the brain that serves a purpose and then dissolves into nothingness when those impulses die. But consciousness does not submit itself so easily to this sort of reductionist analysis, not least because it is itself the progenitor of reductionism, the scientific method and reason, and never proves itself to be less than the whole of the knowledge it seeks to acquire. Consciousness is never less than co-extensive with the world. In this interdependent relationship of the knower and the known, the material world appears as the unstable and changing form of the external object of knowledge, and that which knows appears as the unchanging and unmoving fulcrum around which the changing and moving world revolves. One is impermanent matter, the other permanent immateriality: the immortal soul of Plato that returns to its mortal body, the spirit of Descartes that outlasts it.

In the *samkhya* doctrine, which forms the philosophical foundation of the core teaching of the *Gita*, the nature and the presence of each of these two factors, the material and the immaterial, are explained as *prakriti* and *purusha*. *Prakriti* is fundamental unformed matter. *Purusha* is the 'original person', usually translated as 'spirit'. Both are seen as the complementary founding elements of the cosmos from which all created beings are descended. From *prakriti* we derive our material nature – the body, senses, motivations, locomotion and, significantly, the mind. *Purusha* is that sense of the 'original person' or resident self in the body that refuses to be explained merely by the formal nature of the material organism. This philosophy therefore proposes, quite rationally and by no means uniquely, the pre-existence of both matter and spirit to account for the existence of material beings and their ever-changing forms, constantly recreated from undifferentiated matter, and the continual recurrence of the 'person' embodied in those material forms of being.

One of the important contributions of this doctrine as it appears in the *Gita* that will ultimately help us to understand the concept of the self and why it will come to be seen as cognate with *brahman*, is to have situated the mind among other material qualities of being. The mind (*manas*) is an organ of the body. Man shares with all other living creatures both a material form and a range of material interests given by material nature. His material nature is not of his own willing but is given in the impersonal and unknowable ground of being. All creatures are driven by virtue of that same ground of being to sustain their organic integrity and to seek out their own interests, both as individuals and as species. They find nourishment in the biosphere; they compete for food and for space; they reproduce their own kind; their sensory organs respond to external stimuli; their innate instinctive desires drive them to satisfy their various appetites. Organs of hearing, sight, smell, taste and touch help define their sphere and limits of action; their physiological attributes, their limbs, hands, tentacle, claws, teeth, tongues, facilitate the actions motivated by the desires initiated in their individual sensory domains. The mind is another, higher co-ordinating material organ capable of recognising the forms of the body's external interests in the world, and representing the shape of its internal desires, hopes, fears and motives. The mind co-ordinates the inner and the outer for the satisfaction of the whole organism's material needs and the fulfilment of its instinctive will to live. In common with other organs, it is in essence entirely functional.

In some of the more difficult technical passages in the *Gita*, the material body and its sphere of activity is called the 'field' (13:0-13:6). This objective 'field of action' parallels the 'field' of action that is the battlefield background of the narrative, and the word in Sanskrit, *kshetre*, is the same in each instance. The 'field', as it is described in these verses, is compounded of the gross material elements that were thought to account for all animate and inanimate objects: earth, air, fire, water and the more mysterious 'aether', which, as the supposed invisible conductor of light, was an essential element of scientific theories about the nature of the material universe well into the nineteenth century. The organs of sensation, and the organs the body possesses to accomplish all its actions, along with the mind through which sensations and calls to action are mediated, are all considered components of the field. The field, this theory argues, has the power to sustain itself as an organic unit. Its nature is changeable – it has its moods, emotions, desires, hurts and pleasures. It is also, as the material body, host to the intelligence and to the mind's construction of the ego that sees itself as the agent of all the actions that unfold in the field.

But the ego-self is the product of material nature, a made-up 'I' (*ahamkaras*), a functional construct to account to itself for the actions that are in the first place the domain of the senses and the bodily organs, and secondly the promptings of the self-will of the organism and its appetites. We may improve our perspective on this sometimes elusive argument by stepping back from our human and ego-centred position to consider the whole of the material world, both organic and inorganic, on its own ground or merit. Everything in the world, we now know, is in action. Fire burns at the heart of the earth, the seas are in tumult, the wind whips through the mountains, and not even the rocks are still but are held together by atomic forces, by moving particles. At both the microcosmic and the macrocosmic level, strong and weak forces are ceaselessly acting to sustain the integrity of matter and energy. No one is making this happen. Plants have their own anonymous cycles of unconscious being and becoming. Insects and animals go about their business without any awareness of what their business is. The fish does not decide how to spend its day. The bat has its evening mapped out for it. If by some inadvertent and complex genetic mutation the bee were suddenly to acquire a sense of self, this illusory deformation of its sensory apparatus would not change its behaviour in the least, since its patterns of behaviour are already set, given in its hereditary biology. But it might say to itself, in its newly deluded state: 'Look, I have found this patch of clover', when we can see perfectly well that the 'I' was never involved.

The absence of agency is no less true on the human scale despite the resistance of the ego to any attempt to demolish it, for its role is always to defend its own centre of interests. Yet this is not to deny free will. The ego-self is free to choose what it will do, but its choices are determined by its needs and wants, desires and preferences, its preference for the good life over misfortune, a wish to be happy and to avoid pain, a hunger for security and freedom from fear etc, all of which are elements of its material nature defined as the whole 'field' of the body and its attributes. The ego is like the freelance warrior. He is his own man. But he has defined himself as a warrior and is therefore not free of that material construct. He may choose his enemy, but his enemy's enemy is the external source of the reward that will determine his actions. And he may choose his own actions, but they originate from his motives – for money, for reputation or for one form or another of self-gratification. The true agents of action, therefore, are the sensory apparatus and the physiological architecture of the body working in concert with the internal desires, appetites, interests, thoughts, feelings and judgments arising in the body. Together they make up the given character of an individual. The idea of the 'I' that appears to be in charge of its actions is simply that – an idea, resident in the cranium of the individual. When we examine it more closely, what this 'I' turns out to be is the representation of the character already given it. We say, '*I am* such and such a person, *I think* this or *I believe* that, *I like* this or *I dislike* that, these qualities, virtues, faults are *mine.*' And we even go so far as to declare that this body is 'mine' and this life is 'mine'. But all we are doing is defining the ego as something already given. We cannot escape our own character. All our actions simply serve to confirm it. Even if I change 'my' mind about something, it is only a way of finding another route to fulfil the demands of an innate character, as it learns from experience and adapts its behaviour over time.

In the *samkhya* doctrine as it appears in the *Gita*, those traits of character or propensities to act, given in nature, and given irrevocably as the source of individual motives, are known as the *gunas* – literally, 'strands' – that are made to stand for the variable, but essentially non-negotiable dispositions of the character. They are threefold and, though often treated in the *Gita* as isolated one from the other in differing characters, technically they are considered to be interwoven, with one or other dominant in the individual from birth. They are, to use a further analogy, like the strings of the marionette, where the tautness of one string in relation to the others determines the movement of an arm or a leg or the direction of the gaze. The *gunas* (see the Notes on the text, in particular the Note to 7:12) are *rajas*, the powerful, wilful, action-directed character; *tamas*, the indolent opposite character, lacking in will; *sattva*, the 'good' character trying his best to do the right thing. Between them they are intended to explain the varieties of men and their motives and why their actions serve to perpetuate the same characteristic behaviour, repeated from age to age, and hence why, in fact, man's condition itself is unalterable. The self's acts of free will are those already determined by our given character as necessary acts.

Since we have the freedom to act, within the constraints of our innate nature, we are also free not to act. The question that arises very early on in the *Gita* is the extent to which the determination not to act is equally a characteristic of the *gunas* (the *tamasic*, the fearful, the cowardly, the indecisive, on the one hand, or the good *sattvic* character not wishing to do harm, on the other), or whether the self can free itself altogether from the internal motives and external attachments of its innate character by an act of will. If, as individual selves, we can, then clearly there is another 'self' capable of transcending the *gunas*, of denying the necessity to act; a self that can stand on its own ground and recognise, understand and overcome the illusory notion of the 'acting' ego-self engaged in its everyday encounters with the outside world and preoccupied with its interior monologue of hope, desire and anxiety. This self that knows but does not act is referred to in the same verses of the *Gita* that deal with the 'field' (13:0-13:6) as the 'knower of the field'. Action is devolved to the *gunas*, to the character of the 'field' which is the sensory organism itself, the body, mind and ego. That is the entire field of action. The 'knower', the self, does not act. It is the witness, the watcher, the observer, the spectator:

> *This, the body's highest*
> *immaterial resident,*
> *is called the witness or observer,*
> *the permitter, the supporter,*
> *the experiencer,*

the greater ruler and the supreme self. (13:22)

It knows its own actions, knows its own emotions, understands its own motives, but at the same time also knows that these are not really its 'own' but simply how its material nature is constituted. A man may smile or a man may cry, just as a dog may bark or wag its tail. They are part of the way things are. To the self that 'knows' they are characteristics of *what* it knows; they are not anything to which the self is attached, but one observable and observed thing followed by another.

The self is the personal, subjective obverse of impersonal, objective *brahman*. *Brahman* is the ground or principle of being that does not act. *Brahman* is not agency:

I do nothing of myself
through all eternity. (4:13)

The self, too, 'does nothing' (13:29). The self is the ground of knowledge, not of action. Both the self and *brahman* are unattached to and untouched by actions, which are attributable to material nature and the *gunas*. *Brahman* is the 'thatness' of the world in itself. The self is the 'thisness' of subjective being. To know the self as the 'knower' and to know that it is not the agent of action but the witness of the influence of the *gunas* that give rise to the bodily self's motives and consequent actions, is the highest form of knowledge:

True knowledge is to know
the field and know the knower. (13:2)

With this perspective in mind we can return to the opening of the *Bhagavad Gita* and to Arjuna and his dilemma in the field of action, whose actions are not of his willing, and how the problem of moral action is developed and resolved.

It is a common practice among interpreters of the *Gita* to pass over the difficulties, inconsistencies and contradictions of the text – a text of many voices derived from multiple sources – when those anomalies are in conflict with a preferred 'spiritual' reading of the verses that would make them a harmonious whole. Nowhere is this more evident than in the 'problem' of the actual war setting and how this is to be reconciled with the theme of love or devotion in the *Gita* upon which that wishful interpretation tends to be founded. Mascaró, in the introduction to his 1962 rendering of the text, says quite baldly: 'If we want to understand the spiritual meaning of the *Bhagavad Gita*, we had better forget everything concerning the great battle of the *Mahabharata* or the story of Krishna and Arjuna in the vast epic.' The poem is to be seen as a 'vast symphony' of spiritual themes in which the 'stirring sounds' of the battle are but one, for this is a 'great battle for an inner victory, and the despairing cry of the soul ready to give up the struggle.' This recasting of the moral context of the dialogue as allegory for an inner conflict has also been adopted, if a little more apologetically, by Easwaran, a decision reflected in the title given to his translation of Book 1 as 'The War Within'. The sentiment has its precedent in Gandhi who expressed the view, speaking in 1926, that while the *Gita* acknowledged violence in the world it did not provide justification for it. The battle, in this view, is 'a conflict within the human body between opposing moral tendencies imagined as distinct figures.' This figurative approach to the opening of the *Gita*, by removing the real moral problem of action, agency, responsibility and guilt from the actual field of action, presents us with an allegorical field in which good and evil, vice and virtue, ignorance and wisdom contend as representative persons, yet lacking any textual key to the fable that would allow us to read the *Gita* as a sort of Indian *Pilgrim's Progress*. Certainly there is a spiritual awakening at stake if we were to misrepresent the purport of the *Gita* as a justification for violence and war. On the contrary, the reality of physical violence and death in a war setting, marking the farthest reaches of human moral conflict, provides the context for the radical disillusionment that will lead Arjuna to question his actions.

Readers of the *Gita* are struck by the incongruous disruption of the *Mahabharata* narrative at this point; why this long interlude, a Q&A dialogue and compilation of spiritual instruction, is inserted here at a critical moment in the impending conflict, and ostensibly carried on right in the middle of the battlefield between two opposing armies. But it is precisely because it *is* a critical moment, a point of no return, that it is thematically the right place to begin the argument. There can be no more extreme situation in which to bring into focus the morality of our actions and the internal conflict between duty and conscience than when face-to-face with death and the necessity to act in the name of death, where to act is to kill or be killed. For a battle-hardened warrior such as Arjuna, this circumstance alone does not create in his mind a crisis of conscience. That crisis is contrived in the *Gita* by having Arjuna recognise that his actions will result in the death of his own kinsmen and the corruption of the social order that must follow. It is this realisation that triggers his reluctance to act, and it is his refusal to act that then allows the dialogue on the subject of action, non-action and agency to unfold. Krishna does not directly address Arjuna's specific problem of conscience, but speaks of death and deathlessness as though the problem were the fear of death. But Arjuna does not express any fear of death. His fear is guilt; and we overcome guilt, Krishna will argue, by realising we are not the agent of our actions but the instrument of actions provoked by various passions which we can learn to transcend, and by attachments of self-interest from which we can become free.

All the ills of the world arise from the actions of men

seeking to change the order of things, from good as well as evil motives. All evils, wrote Machiavelli, quoting Sallust, 'have their origin in good beginnings.' The moral strength of the good is in resisting the impulse to act for the good by violent and evil means. We can never truly act for the good because good motives carry no guarantee to confer good consequences on our actions. To avoid evils we must refrain from action. But if we cannot act for the good we must act to resist evil. Not acting has its consequences too. It may be sufficient for a man to give up his life rather than act against the incursion of evil into the peaceful equanimity of his existence, but he cannot sacrifice the lives of others on his behalf. There comes a time when we have no choice but to act, to defend the lives of our children, our family, our comrades, our people. Defeat without resistance is absolute.

Arjuna lays down his bow and refuses to fight in a decision not to act made from the depths of his conscience. But the evil consequences he fears cannot be evaded by his own refusal to act. The action has begun, and one army or the other will prevail, men and kings and princes will die, and the disintegration of the extended family at war with itself will follow regardless. Defeat is defeat, however it comes about. This point of crisis at the moment of engagement between two contending forces, each believing it has right on its side, has been reached through a connected series of causes and effects with its beginnings in the motives of the participants and the motivating impulses of man's innate nature. Actions do not spring simply from greed, ambition and enmity, but also from a sense of nobility and righteousness. This admixture of qualities (the *gunas* are often translated as 'qualities') nonetheless makes up a pool of characteristics that determines an individual's behaviour. Together, these characteristics contribute to, in effect, one single motivation: the preservation and promotion of self-interest, of 'me' and 'mine', with every resultant act designed to ensure the welfare of this singular biological unit of being and the security of its sphere of interest, but in doing so attaching it blindly and unquestioningly to its material existence.

This biological singularity of the person, however, does not stand alone. We are not quite the individual autonomous creatures we think we are. To be at all, we must accept a prior dependency on the material and biological nature of others who came before us (ourselves in other guises). We are who we are by virtue of all that has preceded us. We are none of us a miraculously conceived original. We conform to a pattern – physiologically and psychologically, materially and mentally – whose design was laid out before we ever came to be. We might say that to be who we are we must first conform exactly to what we are not. We are 'other' well before we acquire the least intimation of being who we think we are. The 'other' lays down the rules of behaviour and we conform to them. We can see this most clearly at work in nature. We observe the physical constraints imposed on an animal by its physiological pattern and the limits of its behaviour imposed on it by that physiology. The dog wags its tail in one direction for appeasement, the other way to indicate aggression; it bares its teeth; it fights, it marks its territory, it barks, it bites. It has no wings to fly, no sting in its tail, no voice to argue or persuade. Each creature conforms to its own nature, and its nature is pre-defined by the limits of its being and its actions. What results, cumulatively, from these many and varied individual natures in instinctive pursuit of their own survival and wellbeing, is the great abundance and diversity of life forms we see all around us, each contending for space, air, nourishment, for continuity – all of it willed elsewhere in the inherited patterns of material being. Out of this perpetual conflict and competition, bloody and destructive, in which everything in the end dies but is born again to continue the struggle, comes order. Everything dies, and creatures destroy themselves, but order always prevails.

We may retreat in horror from some aspects of nature memorably described by Tennyson as 'red in tooth and claw', but we must acknowledge that such patterns of behaviour have been tried and tested in the crucible of evolution and that they exist because they work, and they prevail because life itself prevails. The world of nature has its 'moral' order if we define moral order as the establishment and perpetuation of order in species, populations or communities through the incorporated 'correct' (if not entirely palatable) behaviours of individual organisms within them.

Even the rudiments of what we would call moral *judgment* can also be shown to have been given in instinct, entirely without the benefit of moral *reasoning*. A growing body of evidence from studies in ethology, sociobiology and ecology has demonstrated at least some superficial connection between instinctive social behaviours and what we call in ourselves moral judgments. Animals as diverse as brown bears, stags and sticklebacks make 'judgments' about when to attack and when to retreat in confrontational situations where that judgment balances aggressive territorial imperatives against the likelihood of success in facing off an inferior or superior opponent. But they might fight to the death if they have everything to lose. Animals from domestic hens to wolves, from ants to chimpanzees, 'co-operate' when their self-interests are mutual. The dominant hen that this morning stole the food put out for the other one, nevertheless settles down after dark in its secondary place in the nest to get warmth from its rival. Animals seem to understand 'fairness', the basic principle that you can't go on for ever dealing out blows to another without some day bringing those same blows upon yourself when the situation changes. Even the last hen in the pecking order gets to eat, for who knows when the first shall be last? Not going too far is one way of increasing the chances of survival when the tables are turned, a sort of instinctive bartering that prevents a rush to one-way destruction by which no one's interest is served. Self-interests even themselves out in the interests of wolves, hens, chimps and people in general, and not just in the interests of one (mortal) individual. In these behavioural scenarios, who ultimately benefits from the moral judgment of the individual? Not the individual organism itself, for the organism dies. It expends its life in the instinctive pursuit of its perpetuation. It is, in fact, expendable, for what it perpetuates is not its own life but the integrity of the social order, or the colony or, in the final analysis, the species that gave rise to it. For it is the species itself that determines the behaviour of the individual, which can only act within the limits of the physiology and the instinctive or intuitive behavioural pattern bequeathed it.

Are human moral judgments so very different? We easily recognise in ourselves the instinctive drives for food, warmth and shelter. We experience anger and frustration when our desires are thwarted. We defend the interests of ourselves, our families, our homes, our property, our possessions. We also 'know' what is right and what is wrong: that it is right to be fair and just, right to co-operate with and help others; and that it is wrong to steal, to cheat, to injure, to kill. And although all those moral judgments are mediated by the mind and its capacity for reason, they are in essence similar to the inherited intuitions of prohibitions and permissions that regulate the mutual, interdependent relationships between all individuals and societies in the biosphere. We have, of course, socialised rules for behaviour that are learned, and laws of behaviour that are imposed, but we also have an inherent moral sense that limits the harm we can do to ourselves and to others, in the interests of the whole, and upon which those rules and laws are founded.

In a time of war, the rules of moral behaviour designed to balance the mutual interests of civil society are transformed into rules that support the integrity of the social order and society's overriding interest in the exercise of its power. Then the individual must exchange friendship for enmity, peaceability for aggression, and prohibitions for permissions. He may now destroy property, injure others, take without giving and kill with impunity. He must also be prepared to offer up his own life. For what? For something other than himself, for something not of his own willing or his own choosing.

How powerful indeed are the blind forces at work in each person, working against his will, overwhelming the individual and his conscience. The causes of the crisis to which Arjuna has been brought on the Kuru field have their roots in the instinctive struggle for power and domination, property and wealth, motivated by self-interest, greed, ambition on the one hand, by righteousness on the other: we have all heard of 'just' wars and wars 'for peace'. It is too late, face to face with the enemy, to begin a moral debate on the rightness of actions about to unfold inevitably as the result of other actions already taken, actions driven by those unresistable motivating forces of material nature and our own innate character. The rules are written for us, biologically, physiologically, psychologically, behaviourally, socially, morally. To act morally is simply to act in accordance with law and with duty, since these are both given in the moral order of the whole of which each individual is a part. The integrity of the whole is maintained if each plays his true part. The social order we encounter in the *Gita* is the immutable order of the Aryan caste system, which is sustained by each performing with integrity his inherited role (his *dharma*) without encroaching on the duty of another:

> *Better your own duty,*
> *though imperfect,*
> *than another's duty well-performed.*
> *Better death in your own calling*

than inviting harm by undertaking
duties that belong to others. (3:35)

Arjuna, the warrior of *kshatrya* caste, must fight. His actions
are not his to own. He is a player, a character in an unfolding
drama whose causes, motives and, ultimately, whose
denouement are all given already in the action itself. Arjuna
is not the agent of his actions, and nor is he the conscience of
those actions precipitated by laws of material nature beyond
his reach and comprehension.

So who is Arjuna, the man who is conscience-stricken,
full of doubt, immobilised and dejected on the field of duty
(*dharmakshetre*), if he is not the actor, not the agent of his
actions, not the conscience of his actions, but a mere puppet
of universal laws of cause and effect, for neither he nor we
have the wooden heads and hollow hearts of a marionette?

The cycle of life and death, the coming into being
of individual organisms and their dissolution into the stuff
of matter, their self-sustaining imperatives to live and
their ultimate systemic failure as self-sufficient units, is a
phenomenon of the material world and its physical 'laws'.
An organism performing its work cycle, going through
the motions of its lifecycle, is an autonomous agent, but
its autonomy only serves to complete that cycle; it is
not autonomous in any other way, just as a steam engine
might be said to be the agent of its locomotion though its
whole purpose and principle is already given in the laws of
thermodynamics. The organism is not a 'free' agent but is
bound by its lifecycle. It is only free so far as it is able to make
judgments that will permit the fulfilment of the commands
of its own nature to live and not perish.

The limits of man's freedom are harder to discern
because, as conscious beings, there has arisen in us a sense of
a self – self-consciousness – an 'I', an ego which is the focus of
all our interests as a self-sustaining, and now self-regarding,

organism. The animal looks out into a world that is always in the present. It does not reflect on the past or fret about the future. Its life simply unfolds and its actions are the signs of its unfolding. But we *know* what we want, and we know the anxiety of not yet having what we want and we act in order to get it – we act to make a living, to find food, shelter, comfort and happiness – and it is the illusion of the 'self' at the centre of 'self-interest' that appears to us to be doing the acting. But if the self is the agent, then properly conceived the self is agent in one sense only: as one appointed by another to do his bidding. What I do, and the limits of what I am able to do, are determined by the nature of my being and the necessity of meeting the contingencies of a life already given in nature.

Yet the self is *something* and *someone*. I know that I am the product of external contingencies, that I live and grow and die. And yet *I am*:

> *Through childhood, youth and age*
> *I am, though all these pass.*
> *Just so, my body passes on*
> *and yet I am.* (2:13)

The 'I am' knows only what it is to be. It knows its own thoughts and feelings, its own pains and pleasures, and it knows its actions. But it does not know birth and it does not know death, for these are not subjects of experience. They are both externalities, the forms of material nature appearing and disappearing as phenomena. The 'I am' does not know, and can never know, what it is to be the 'I am not'. And all those anxieties, ambitions, ambiguities, satisfactions and disappointments of a life can also be seen, from a higher vantage point, as the adventures and misadventures of a material existence merely observed as phenomena. If we could detach ourselves from them, they might seem to us simply as something we *know*, and not something that in essence we *are*. Completely detached from materiality we can only *know* and only *be*. The self that knows, the self severed from the idea of itself, from 'me' and 'mine', knows only pure being. That sense of pure being is both unique to the individual, embodied in his material self, and universal, since it resides as the universal self in every being, untainted by the body's material nature, its actions and the delusions of the self as ego and agent. The self of pure being is referred to constantly in the *Gita* as the purified self, which we can discover by stripping away all the trappings of the material life in which it is embodied:

> *he purifies the self...*
> *and becomes the self*
> *within the self*
> *of every being.* (5:7)

The self is always present. It knows neither birth nor death. So in this sense it is both unborn and immortal, outside time. Bodies, we can easily see, are timebound and subject to birth and death. But the self knows only the self, being knows only being; there is no time at which we do not know what it is to be:

> *Nowhere will you find*
> *not-being.*
> *Being is all that can be found.* (2:16)

From the perspective of eternity, which is the self's standpoint, life is given and taken away in the same instant, as the necessary condition of material being, but the embodied self, the 'endlessness within', is never absent. In the *Gita*, on the field of battle, we are assured:

> *In truth, there never was a time*
> *when I was not,*
> *and never will there be a time*
> *when I shall cease to be,*
> *nor a time for you,*
> *nor for all these lords of men.* (2:12)

If the 'true', but yet to be disclosed self (for it is tangled up in the illusion of the self as agency) is the indestructible 'embodied' self, then the 'true' Arjuna cannot be destroyed. But nor can he destroy others, for they too are embodied selves and their material lives, their bodies, are already given and taken away as the fateful condition of all contingent beings, including the contingent actions imposed on them and on Arjuna. The self does not act. The self is the subject of being and knowing, not the agent of acting and doing, for action belongs to the objective world, to the 'field', and not to that which knows the world, the 'knower of the field'.

    If the self is not the agent, but sits still doing nothing, as it were, at the centre of the action; if it cannot 'own' its actions but only 'know' the actions mediated by the ego-self of material nature (the self as a bundle of sensations and motivations that lead to the execution of actions under the influence of those impulses); then the self is not only not the responsible agent of action but it is also not the guilty party in the unfolding of any of those actions. Strictly speaking, the self, by transcending actions it had previously attributed to its own agency, is beyond both good and evil. 'Guilt does not mark him' (5:10). The moral order of a man's actions is embedded in the intuitive understanding of right and wrong actions, and in the social constraints imposed on the individual's scope for action by the social body as a whole. The statement that the self is free from guilt is easily misunderstood. It seems to imply that the enlightened self, or the 'wise man', can act with impunity, and certainly that has often been a position taken by the Brahmin. But the self *does not act*. So this is simply a statement of fact: if the self does not act it cannot be guilty of an act. Wisdom does not exempt a wise man from responsibility, and no one has the right to claim to be 'above' moral considerations. As soon as such a man acts, from either good or evil motives, or for good or evil ends, he simply falls back into the trap of his ego-attachment to ends and means, the victim of his arrogant character and the vanity of mistaking knowledge and learning for wisdom and insight. In the *Gita* teaching, to avoid guilt in a material world in which our natures are ordered by the *gunas*, one must adhere to the *dharma*, to the duty, of one's birth into that world and its immutable order:

> *Actions that arise*
> *from one's own nature*
> *incur no guilt.* (18:47)

Conscience is linked to duty and its fulfilment, guilt to its neglect.

When we are born, we are born into a world that already exists to receive us. The world is new to us, but we are not new to it. As we come into the world, so others leave it; but the order of the world itself is not much disturbed by this. We are like stones on the beach, brought in and washed out on the tide, jostled in and out of position – but there is always a pebbly beach. From generation to generation everyone dies, everyone is born – or reborn. And why not reborn? Wherever we look, someone is labouring in the fields, someone selling flowers or selling tea, someone digging a hole in the road, another setting off to be a soldier, or to work in the factory, or to open up the shop. Everything is different, yet everything is the same. Just as the cells in our bodies are not the same cells we were born with, yet we are conscious of being the same person, bodies are different reconstructions but they are the same bodies. We don't need a theory of the transmigration of souls, or the role of fire and smoke in their translation from one world to another (see 8:23-8:25), in order to acknowledge the inexorable cycle of birth and death without end that only perpetuates the same condition. We live, we work, we die; we remember who we are and then we forget; and the cycle continues, from nothingness to being, from being to nothingness. Does the 'we' of this cycle really matter if the self that mediates this lifecycle is just a material component of that cycle, and if the 'true' self embodied in its present manifest form is immortal and indestructible? 'We' come and go, the anonymous creatures of time, but 'I' am ever-present.

Every born creature is constrained in its nature and its actions by being born as something in particular. Whatever has gone on in the past to differentiate the turtle, living peaceably in that intermediate region between the sea and the land, and the tiger, ferocious in the forest; to create a man or a woman, a good person or a wicked one; to require so many worker ants and so many soldier ants to maintain the colony; wherever those origins may lie in the past, as chance or necessity, accident or inevitability, the existence of every being is determined by its birth, and when it is born it is what it is and cannot be otherwise. In the *Gita*, the social order of the caste system is as immutable as the natural order. The past has already determined the present. You may have been something else in a past life, and you *might* have been something else in this one, but you are what you are: a Brahmin, a woman, an elephant, a dog. A dog, clearly, cannot be an elephant or behave like one or take on the tasks (or tusks) of one. Equally, a woman cannot be a Brahmin. You don't escape your condition by revolting against it, nor by taking on the role or duties of another. We must accept our status as the determined condition of being. We must act with complete integrity in the performance of our determined duty – we must fulfil our *dharma*. By following our *dharma* we are true to ourselves and true to our duty in the social order. Any amelioration of our status will arise, in future lives, from the integrity of our actions in this one. Our present lives will become our past lives, determining our future lives. To refuse or resist our *dharma* is to disturb the stability of the order of society, to introduce chaos into order, and to set up a chain of consequences that can only lead to a deterioration of status in a future life and to the decline of the social order itself. Moral actions, therefore, are simplified in this account as actions appropriate to and integral to the fulfilment of one's *dharma*. These are true and right actions – bearing in mind that the word '*dharma*' also carries the weight of 'truth', 'righteousness' and 'law'.

We know what is meant by goodness in the *Gita* from the three 'austerities' of the *sattvic* or 'good' character: the austerities or restraints of the body, speech and mind. They include respect, virtue, self-control, non-violence, truthfulness, inoffensiveness, tranquillity, benevolence and silence (see 17:14-17:17). But these are qualities of the individual character, to be esteemed and promoted. The social and economic structure of the caste system is neither inherently good nor inherently bad. No political or economic social order ever is. It is first and foremost the form of order. 'Good' or 'bad' arise not from good or bad government but from the justice or injustice of men's actions, from virtue or the lack of it. We have had more than two thousand years since the creation of the *Bhagavad Gita*, and two thousand years of Christian virtue in the civilisation of the West, to learn that revolutions in the social order of society have done nothing to permanently change the character of the individual or to bring society closer to godliness. As social animals we cannot escape our mortal condition or our role, one way or another, in the social order, whether as prince and ruler, vagabond or outcaste. But the self, the true self, is not the actor in this fateful drama of life. The self does not act. It is the observer, in its bodily incarnation, of its fatefulness. The material nature of the body is given, the character of the ego-self is given, the mind and the intellect are given, the social order is given, the moral order of society is given, death is given. The self is manifest in a material world of change and death. Yet the self is deathless and unchanging. But in everyday life it is mired in its delusions and tangled in its attachments to the material world and the material interests of the ego-self, engrossed in its own motivated actions, its labours and its pursuit of happiness. The self is lost, unable to differentiate the self as pure subjective being from the subjective representation of the forms of its interests and actions.

For that self to find itself, something needs to happen, something needs to give way; an act of will is required; and the spur for that act of will almost invariably arises from a crisis of conscience, or from the sudden collapse of all the comforting illusions of life which have protected us from the realisation of the tragic nature of being, of living and dying, from the pointlessness of the same earthly round without sublimation. Arjuna's internal crisis, in the *Gita* section of the *Mahabharata* epic, has presented the opportunity to differentiate the sources of action in the material order of the body and mind, and in the moral order of the social organisation, from the non-acting self. What then follows, if we track the main current of the argument through the text, is a succession of teachings that describe how the self can be liberated from its inherited condition by rejecting all attachment to that condition, and discover a continuity coterminous with the universe itself. Along the way, the *Gita* discusses and dismisses a number of alternative and widely adopted, but fruitless, paths to self-liberation.

To discover the self is to deny the self, the ego-self locked into its material condition. The *Gita* provides an intellectual framework for understanding what the denial of the self entails: the necessity of both acquiring a body of transmitted knowledge or wisdom (*jnana*) and of following a disciplined method to achieve that understanding in practice (*yoga*) that will lead to self-realisation and freedom. Without that understanding, the logic of self-denial by suppressing the natural urges of the material self and subduing the senses in one's body leads to various austerities and ascetic practices, common in the centuries up to the time of the *Gita* and through the period of development of the *samkhya* philosophy, and still prevalent today. The Buddha himself practised these forms of self-denial and self-mortification before discovering the 'middle way' of an intellectual understanding combined with disciplined meditative practice leading to enlightenment and the annihilation of the illusion of the ego-self. Greek philosophers in the time of Alexander encountered the gymnosophists of India, naked and baked by the hot sun, who, by practising extreme self-torture, hoped to demonstrate how far above their material incarnation they had ascended. All these forms of ascetic practices are severely condemned in the *Gita*, both as unnatural ways to conduct oneself in the world (3:5-3:6), and as just another form of egotism (17:5).

The rites and sacrifices of the vedic religion are treated in the same way. While the *Gita* shows a certain distanced degree of respect for the whole class of 'austerities' which mark man's search for something higher than his earth-bound self, including the rites and sacrifices of religion and worship, it recognises them as essentially aspects of man's fearful and egotistical nature; they are not true spiritual ways to insight and redemption, but methods to realise benefits either in this world or the next, in this life or another:

> *These are men*
> *whose minds are rooted in desire,*
> *intent on heaven*
> *and securing their rebirth,*
> *meticulous in their performance of the rites*
> *to bring them powers and pleasures.* (2:43)

The true 'austerity' is the austerity of wisdom:

> *Many kinds of offerings*
> *are laid before the face of brahman.*
> *All these are motivated actions.*
> *Know this and be free.*
> *The offering of wisdom*
> *is better than material*
> *sacrifices,*
> *for all these*
> *are resolved in wisdom.* (4:32-4:33)

The *Gita* teaches that, for one who understands, the rites and sacrifices have no value:

> *All the rites*
> *have no more value*
> *to the wise*
> *than water in a well*
> *when all the world*
> *is full to overflowing.* (2:46)

They are grouped with other ritual practices which all rely on one external agency or another to rescue a man from his fate, improve his lot or ensure his translation from his mortal state to another. The worship of gods, or spirits and demons, and ancestor worship – all ancient practices of primitive religion – are dismissed in one breath:

Those who worship the gods
go to the gods
and those devoted to the ancestors
go to them.
Those who put their faith in goblins
have their goblin world,
but the one who loves me
comes to me. (9:25)

The wise, the men of disciplined understanding who follow the *yoga* of wisdom, understand the true nature of the self, and in doing so understand the true object of devotion.

There is no understanding without discipline, without effort. The self must make the effort – to escape the self and to realise the self:

The self should raise
the self
and not let down
the self. (6:5)

The self is both the friend and enemy of the self, its aid – by making the effort to release itself from its illusions – or the obstacle in its way by remaining enmeshed in its illusions, insistent that they represent the 'all' of life and its fulfilment, 'the all of everything, without a larger view of causes' (18:22). The effort is to be made from within the resources of one's material nature, with the power of one's intelligence or will (*buddhi*). While the self is busy looking after its own interests, with its head down, with its shoulder to the wheel, it has no reason to look up, no incentive to cease its labours. It can only discover itself by making the effort to leave behind its preoccupation with the essential tasks of making a living and pursuing health, wealth, success and happiness, the rewards of which are not lasting, and try to understand and thereby reveal its everlasting inner nature.

You can't drift along in *tamasic* laziness, keep striving onwards with *rajasic* energy, or maintain a permanent balance as a good and fair *sattvic* person, without confirming just what you are by continuing to do just what you do. And you can't easily overcome the habits of your own nature and character unless you acquire an understanding of the true nature of the self, and that understanding can't be achieved without effort. Practice itself, the practice of all forms of austerities, including the practice of meditation and concentration, without the goal of understanding, is just practice, and is ultimately self-deluding:

> *There is no understanding*
> *without the discipline of self-control*
> *and no attempt at it*
> *without determined effort,*
> *and where there is no effort*
> *nor is there abiding peace of mind.*
> *And how can anyone be happy*
> *unquiet in his mind?* (2:66)

Shankara very wisely commented that 'the effort required is not for the knowledge of either *brahman* or the self, but only to prevent us from mistaking the not-self for the self.' The *yoga* discipline referred to throughout the *Gita* is aimed at subduing the senses, the stimulus created in the body and the mind by the sensory world, and the impulse to act as a result of that stimulus. Its objective is to detach the self from its desires and its motives, and ultimately to recognise the non-acting self as the tranquil, undisturbed and imperturbable 'witness' of the world. In its pure form of 'knowledge-discipline', *jnana-yoga* appears to be the older of the two schools of *yoga* which the *Gita* challenges in its reasoned explanations of the teaching of the *karma-yoga* school. The doctrine of pure knowledge-discipline is practised by those who, focusing all their attention on detaching the self from the desires and motives that lead to action in the material world of the senses, also divorce themselves from the world itself and remove any need or obligation to act in it or have any other role in the social order than that of the *sadhu* or mendicant, dependent on alms and the gifts of those who do act in the world but respect the holiness of those who are able to detach themselves from it. From the outset, the *Gita* takes a different view.

It is impossible not to act. We have to perform our natural bodily functions. We must act simply in order to live. And we need not look farther for evidence than the fact that the world continues to revolve, and is endlessly active in the maintenance of its own integrity. We are of the nature of things. But the self is outside the action. There is no need to divorce the self from the world of action, because it really has no part to play in it when the sources of action are properly understood. The *karma-yoga* philosophy propounded in the *Gita* accepts the world as it is, and on its own undisclosed ground of being (*brahman*). It recognises that the eternal round of the material forms of being is driven by the tenacity with which those forms hold on to their material condition. Nothing can escape that condition except that which is already free of it: the unborn and undying, immaterial, unrealised (but realisable) self.

In the *Gita* the 'I' or the 'I am' speaks, as Walt Whitman speaks, on behalf of the universal self, the eternal soul, and simultaneously on behalf of the universe, as though the universe itself were entirely suspended in a subjective consciousness 'infinite and omnigenous'.[1]

---

[1] Whitman, Walt. *Song of Myself* (line 698).

> *I am the same self in all beings*
> *and neither love one nor despise another.* (9:29)

The 'I am' of the self 'hidden in illusion', the 'I am' that is 'unborn and undying' (7:25) is one with the fragrance and the taste of the universe:

> *I am the taste*
> *of the waters.*
> *I am the radiance*
> *of the sun and moon.* (7:8)

The 'I' is both subject and object:

> *I am the eternal witness*
> *and material cause*
> *of all things animate and inanimate*
> *by which the world exists.* (9:10)

The universe itself is silent. The founding and sustaining principle of the world, *brahman*, is impersonal and purely objective, hidden from us and hidden from itself. It creates everything but does nothing of itself; it is the creative universe on its own ground and not something in the universe acting upon it. The self is viewed in the same way, not as agent acting in and on the field of action, but as the ground of subjective being. There are two inseparable, founding and sustaining principles of the universe, the objective and the subjective: *brahman*, the non-acting objective and unknowable principle of all material existence, and the self, the non-acting subjective principle that knows and speaks, understands and pronounces, and to which, ultimately, *brahman* itself is subordinate. *Brahman* gives rise to the manifest self in its material form, but only the immaterial self, as the knower and witness, can contain it. *Brahman*, which permits the self to be, is forever unknown and unknowable, an infinite and timeless emptiness lost to itself. In return, the self, as subject, is the only permitter of the known and the knowable, of space and time, and of the fullness of the universe forever found and never lost to the 'I am' that knows neither birth nor death. Thus the realisation of the self, detached from its material interests and, indeed, its materiality, is at once the realisation of the self and *brahman*. 'I am' that principle subsumed into myself.

The self detached from action is necessarily free from the moral order of action and from moral responsibility. Without agency there is no one to own actions; actions are the province of the *gunas*, of the will in nature, and of the ego-self through which they are mediated; the rightness or wrongness of those actions and their consequences are measured by their sufficiency to maintain the larger order of self-interest and mutual interest, and the individual's relationship to society, that drives those actions. There is, in the realisation of the self and its unity with *brahman*, only a realisation of aesthetic order, transcending all that we have thought of up to that point as moral order, conscience and duty. The self does not act in the world, it can only know the world. Its only sphere of 'action', therefore, is the field of knowledge, understanding and self-realisation. Its role is 'to be'; and until it realises this state of supreme being, its responsibility is to take steps to become that supreme being. Because we do not see beyond the world of our interests, because we are engrossed in our material needs and wants, because we are attached to what serves our happiness and averse to the sources of unhappiness, because we prefer illusion to the truth, for one is easy and the other hard, the journey towards enlightenment is likely to be a protracted one. The intellectual effort required and the practical effort of self-mastery are difficult and hard to sustain. As with any teaching, it must make provision for small steps which those who are attracted to it can take towards an understanding, and to recommend some practical applications in everyday life that can lead the novice to relinquish the habits of behaviour that tie him to his condition, and set him off on the journey towards light and air and freedom. And each step must have value in itself, for what good will starting out do if we know we do not have the stamina for the journey and may never get there in this lifetime?

Having declared knowledge to be the supreme goal:

> *It is the light of lights*
> *beyond the reach of darkness.*
> *This that must be known*
> *is both the goal of knowledge*
> *and that very knowledge,*
> *dwelling in the hearts of all.* (13:17)

the *Gita* offers some solace to those who will find the direct way to the final goal hard going:

> *I think the final goal*
> *is hard to reach*
> *by one unable to control*
> *the self,*
> *but possible*
> *with proper effort.* (6:36)

for

> *A little effort,*
> *even, is not lost,*
> *nor does it lessen.* (2:40)

We can make a start by turning away from a preoccupation

with our inherited condition towards something higher and beyond it, yet within us. If the goal of knowledge is the highest and the hardest of these efforts, some peace of mind, the *Gita* advocates (see throughout Book 12), can be achieved through meditation, and the subjugation of the senses and their distractions reached through *yoga* practice – sitting still and controlling the desires that arise in the mind. One can also practise renunciation, abandoning both the motivation to want things, and the things themselves that are the objects of those wants and wishes. Failing that, simply acting with restraint will set you on the right path. And, finally, it teaches faith, it teaches surrender to the highest object of devotion. But how we interpret what is meant by the highest object of devotion, or even whether we may see the act of devotion without a goal as sufficient in itself, will depend on how well we are able to follow the contending voices of the *Gita* and distinguish the teaching itself as the goal from the figure of its 'divine' giver.

Faith is the great leveller when the understanding fails. The word is sown among thorns, among 'the cares of this world, and the deceitfulness of riches, and the lusts of other things entering in'.[1] For a man's vision is his own and cannot easily be transmitted except by imperfect stages and attempts, by parable and exhortation, and in the end must be taken on faith. From a rational point of view, faith is the last resort, but for the faithful it is the first and unfailing resort. The three foundations of Christianity are Jesus as the teacher aflame with his eschatological vision of the end of time; the 'gospel' or teaching of the soul's return to God by turning away from wickedness and earthly desires towards the kingdom of heaven within; and the apostolic church through which the teaching is promulgated. The 'three jewels' of Buddhism are the Buddha, as teacher; the *dharma*

---

[1] *St Mark Gospel*, 4:9.

or teaching of the path to enlightenment; and the *sangha*, the discipleship through which the school is established and the teaching perpetuated. Those three elements are paralleled in the *Gita*. The central teaching is given as the doctrine (sometimes referred to as a 'secret doctrine', as in 15:20) of the *samkhya* philosophy, and the 'school' of transmission is that of *samkhya karma-yoga*. If the *samkhya* system has an originator (the sage Kapila is traditionally assigned this role) he is lost to view in the legendary and undocumented distant past. The *yoga* doctrine and its practice are of an ancient lineage, predating Buddhism. That lineage is attested to in the opening verses of Book 4. But there is no personal authority for the teaching in the same way that Jesus is the authority for the Christian gospel and the Buddha for the *dharma*. The core doctrine of the *Gita* exists as a dialogue between master and pupil, as a discourse like the discourses of the Buddha, given by one who knows to one who wishes to understand. The final form of the *Gita* as we have it is substantially overlaid with sentiments of the Vaishnava or Krishna cultists, and the discourse is given to Krishna, lending it the 'divine' authority it otherwise lacks. If we believe the *Gita* as it has come down to us reached its settled form as a response to the encroachment of Buddhism on the authority of the Brahmin and the Brahmin administered religion it for a time usurped, and as a work of the Brahminist revival of the last two centuries BCE, we can easily understand the shift, common to both early Christianity and early Buddhism, from the doctrine to the person of its giver as the object of devotion. In the gospels it is the gospel itself, the 'word', that we are to understand, accept and embrace. The Buddha rejected in his own lifetime and in his own words any suggestion of attachment to his own person – the *dharma* is the objective, the *sangha* the means of reaching it. But the intellectual effort is formidable, and the withdrawal from the field of worldly occupation and the temptations of the flesh required to restore man's soul to himself or to find extinction in Nirvana, is hard to achieve. Faith in the doctrine that leads to the supreme goal gives way to faith in the perfect one, the holy one, who points the way, who *is* the way in his own person. What, after all, is the man to do who hears of the way and delights in the way, but has not the intellectual capacity to understand it (Gandhi insisted the *Bhagavad Gita* was beyond the grasp of the *shudra*); who has ears to hear but who, like the seed fallen among thorns, or like the rich man, cannot extricate himself from his worldly toil, his earthly possessions, his everyday responsibilities; what else is open to him but faith, trust, surrender? For we cannot close the door on him, who believes but falters, sees but does not comprehend, hears but does not understand, tries but fails.

In the *Gita*, the least token of devotion is acceptable:

> *A leaf, a flower,*
> *a fruit, or water*
> *I accept*
> *when offered with devotion*
> *and a pure heart.* (9:26)

This accords with the view that devotion is the *least* that the aspirant to the doctrine can do. Yet it is also made clear that devotion is the *highest* form which that aspiration can take. Arjuna elicits the distinction between the eternal and unmanifest as the object of devotion, and that ideal manifest in the person of Krishna, in the question posed at the opening of Book 12:

> *Which of these*
> *has the better knowledge of the way:*
> *those who steadfastly devote themselves to you*
> *and worship you,*

> *or those who do the same towards*
> *that which is eternal and unmanifest?* (12:1)

It is, of course, to be expected that in those passages interpolated or influenced by the Krishna *bhakti* devotional cult, and those that will bear that interpretation, the worship of Krishna should be portrayed as the highest form of devotion. But I think the origins of the status given to devotion go deeper than this.

If we exclude the obvious Vaishnavite intrusions, such as the bulk of the devotional Books 10 and 11 which are of an entirely different character from the rest of the *Gita*, we find the 'highest object of devotion' described in various, but thematically consistent ways as the self, in its enduring state; the self at one with *brahman*; or as the way of knowledge or wisdom that leads to this state. The self is described objectively in the third person in some parts of the text, and then very frequently speaks for itself in the first person as the subjective unity of *brahman-atman*. (Since the voice that speaks is Krishna's we are at liberty to attribute divine status to Krishna, leaving us with the problem that if Krishna, the 'Lord', is *not* the self, is *not* the expression of *brahman-atman* but is something or someone else, we have two supreme goals and two supreme objects of devotion, one to which the whole *samkhya-yoga* teaching and its doctrine of action and non-action has been tending, and another quite outside it, and contrary to it: an external and divine personage dispensing benevolence and providing a refuge for his devoted worshippers. The two objects cannot be reconciled; they are two separate ideas. The confusion and contradiction that many scholars, translators, interpreters and commentators have read into the *Bhagavad Gita* are simply the result of attempting to marry the declamatory expression of an inner realisation of the self to the conventional idea of a divine external agent who grants it by the power and grace vested in his own person.)

      How wisdom and understanding, the eternal and transcendent self, and the object of worship and devotion come to be seen as one and the same by the 'one who knows' is most fully developed in Book 7, which succeeds in illuminating in one lyrical sequence of verses the goal of wisdom, the self and its relation to *brahman*, the sustaining power of each, and the true nature of worship. Of all those who have faith

> *...the noblest*
> *is the one who knows,*
> *steadfast in his wisdom*
> *and devoted*
> *to this one thing only.* (7:17)

and the one who knows

> *is said to be*
> *myself,*
> *steadfastly abiding in*
> *myself,*
> *the final goal.* (7:18)

The *karma-yoga* teaching, the discipline, knowledge, *brahman*, the self, 'myself', the final goal, and the object of worship and devotion are one:

> *They seek their refuge here in me*
> *who strive towards release*
> *from birth and death.*
> *And they will know these things completely:*
> *the universe in all its power,*
> *the supreme self,*
> *and action.* (7:29)

Those who know me
as the supreme spirit
and as God,
who know me as the highest sacrifice,
even at the hour of death
they know me
and are not perturbed. (7:30)

The self that does not act has no function in the world. It is
not the agent of action, it has no moral responsibility for the
actions of its material nature. It is the eternal witness and
observer, the immaterial heart of every being, the *subject* who
wears the universe itself 'like pearls strung on a thread' (7:7),
for the phenomenal world exists only for the subject. All that
the subject is able to take responsibility for is subjectivity
itself. And there can be no greater responsibility (which is
the poet's and the philosopher's responsibility also) than
consciousness. The self has its duty, its *dharma*, which must
not be confused with its duty as a material and social being.
That *dharma* takes the form of devotion.

This world is such
that action cannot be avoided.
The only action that is free
is worship.
Do this freely. (3:9)

The *Gita* sets out to answer the question of man's moral
nature, the nature of the self and its actions, but in doing
so arrives at the true nature of worship implicit in that
answer: the natural disposition of the self freed from the
delusions of its actions for material ends is to worship, and
devotion, in whatever form it takes, lies therefore in the self's
domain. Worship is our first and only act of freedom. All

other actions are tied to our material condition. All forms of worship, all attitudes of reverence, share something of the self's independence from its material condition and the causes of its actions in the world. Whenever and wherever we deny the binding power of our material nature, and the imperatives of the will in nature which drive our actions, we assert the freedom of the self as subject to create its own world of values, the greatest of which is God.

In Book 16, the *Gita* castigates 'demonic' men who hate the self, the self embodied in every being, and who deny God:

> *They say there is no ground of truth,*
> *no God, no cause or reason in the world...* (16:8)

> *Harnessed to their egos,*
> *to their personal power,*
> *their arrogance, desires and anger,*
> *these ill-thinking men*
> *hate me*
> *embodied in the self*
> *and in the selves of others.* (16:18)

> *These are the worst of men...* (16:19)

The absolute subjectivity of the self *is* God. To deny God is to deny the self. To hate God, to hate the idea of God, is to hate the self and the self in others. To dedicate our lives to the material nature of ourselves that is not ours to own, to believe that 'this is all', and to *wish* that this *should* be all, is a crime against the self. One's worst fate is a godlessness of one's own choosing. Devotion needs no justification or rationalisation – and no object, for devotion itself is the object. It is the affirmation of all values in a material world of eternal recurrence that has no intrinsic value, and the affirmation of the self as the original creator of all values.

BIBLIOGRAPHY

TRANSLATIONS

Wilkins, Sir Charles *The Bhagavat-geeta: Or, Dialogues of Krishna and Arjoon, in Eighteen Lectures : Sanscrit, Canarese, and English, in Parallel Columns*. Bangalore: Wesleyan Mission Press, 1846. [1785]

Thomson, J. Cockburn. *The Bhagavad-Gítá; or A Discourse between Krishna and Arjuna on Divine Matters. A Sanskṛit Philosophical Poem; Translated with Copious Notes, an Introduction on Sanskṛit Philosophy and Other Matter by J. Cockburn Thomson*. Hertford, 1855.

Sastri, A. Mahadeva. *The Bhagavad-Gita with the Commentary of Sri Sankaracharya*. 2nd ed. Mysore, 1901.

Besant, Annie, and Bhagavan Das. *The Bhagavad-gītā with Samskṛt Text, Free Translation into English, an Introduction to Samskṛt Grammar, and a Complete Word-index*. London and Benares: Theosophical Publishing Society, 1905.

Johnston, Charles. *Bhagavad Gita: The Songs of the Master*. Flushing, New York: Charles Johnston, 1908.

Barnett, Lionel D. *Bhagavad-Gita: Or the Lord's Song*. London: J. M. Dent, 1926.

Gandhi, M. K. *The Bhagvadgita*. Delhi: Orient Paperbacks, 1980. [1926]

Hill, W. Douglas P. *The Bhagavad-Gita with English Translation and Commentary*. Winsome Books India, 2004. [1927]

Thomas, Edward. J. *The Song of the Lord: Bhagavadgita*. London: J. Murray, 1931.

Edgerton, Franklin. *Bhagavad Gita*. Part 1: Text and Translation. Cambridge, Massachusetts: Harvard

University Press, 1944.

Edgerton, Franklin. *Bhagavad Gita*. Part 2: Interpretation and Arnold's Translation. Cambridge, Massachusetts: Harvard University Press, 1944.

Prabhavananda, Swami and Christopher Isherwood. *The Song of God: Bhagavad Gita*. 4th ed. Hollywood, CA.: Vedanta Press, 1987. [1944]

Mascaró, Juan. *The Bhagavad Gita*. Harmondsworth, Middlesex: Penguin, 1962.

Zaehner, R. C. *The Bhagavad-Gita: With a Commentary Based on the Original Sources*. Oxford: Clarendon Press, 1969.

Bolle, Keese W. *The Bhagavadgita: A New Translation*. University of California Press, 1979.

Sargeant, Winthrop. *The Bhagavad Gita*. 25th Anniversary ed. Albany, New York: Excelsior Editions, 2009. [1984]

Nabar, Vrinda, and Shanta Tumkur. *The Bhagavadgita*. Ware, Hertfordshire: Wordsworth Classics, 1997.

Mitchell, Stephen. *The Bhagavad Gita: A New Translation*. London: Rider, 2000.

Debroy, Bibek. *The Bhagavad Gita*. Penguin Books India, 2005.

Easwaran, Eknath. *The Bhagavad Gita*. 2nd ed. Tomales, CA: Nilgiri Press, 2007.

Johnson, W. J. *The Bhagavad Gita*. Oxford: Oxford University Press, 2008.

Feuerstein, Georg. *The Bhagavad-Gita: A New Translation*. Boston: Shambhala, 2011.

Flood, Gavin, and Charles Martin. *The Bhagavad Gita*. New York: W. W. Norton, 2015.

SOURCES

Ambedkar, B.R. "Castes of India: Their Mechanism, Genesis and Development." *Indian Antiquary* 41, May 1917.

Basham, A. L. *The Sacred Cow*. Rider, 1990.

Bloomfield, Maurice. *Hymns of the Atharva-Veda, Together with Extracts from the Ritual Books and the Commentaries. Translated by Maurice Bloomfield.* Oxford: Clarendon Press, 1897.

Bouquet, A. C. *Hinduism*. Revised ed. London: Hutchinson University Library, 1962.

Campbell, Joseph. *The Masks of God: Oriental Mythology* New York, NY: Viking Press, 1962.

Chaudhuri, Nirad C. *Hinduism*. London: Chatto & Windus, 1979.

Doniger, Wendy. *The Rig Veda: An Anthology: One Hundred and Eight Hymns, Selected, Translated and Annotated.* Harmondsworth, Middlesex, England: Penguin Books, 1981.

Deussen, Paul. *The Philosophy of the Upanishads*. Edinburgh: T & T Clark, 1906.

Dubois, J. A., and Henry K. Beauchamp. *Hindu Manners, Customs and Ceremonies*. 3rd ed. Oxford: Clarendon Press, 1906.

Griffith, Ralph T. H. *The Hymns of the Rigveda*. Benares, 1889.

Hopkins, Edward Washburn. *The Religions of India*. Boston: Ginn & Company, 1895.

Hume, Robert Ernest. *The Thirteen Principal Upanishads: Translated from the Sanskrit, with an Outline of the Philosophy of the Upanishads, and an Annotated Bibliography.* Oxford University Press, 1921.

Johnson, W. J. *A Dictionary of Hinduism*. Oxford University Press, 2010.

Keith, Arthur Berriedale. *The Samkhya System, a History of the Samkhya Philosophy*. Calcutta: Association Press, 1918.

Keith, Arthur Berriedale. *The Veda of the Black Yajus School Entitled Taittiriya Sanhita*. Cambridge, Massachusetts: Harvard University Press, 1914.

Olivelle, Patrick. *The Law Code of Manu*. Oxford: Oxford University Press, 2009.

Olivelle, Patrick. *Upaniṣads*. Oxford: Oxford University Press, 1996.

Sharpe, Eric J. *The Universal Gita: Western Images of the Bhagavadgita: A Bicentenary Survey*. London: Duckworth, 1985.

Walker, Benjamin. *Hindu World: An Encyclopedic Survey of Hinduism in Two Volumes*. London: Allen & Unwin, 1968.

Wheeler, Sir Mortimer. *The Indus Civilization*. 3rd ed. Cambridge University Press, 1968.

Zaehner, R. C. *Hindu Scriptures*. Everyman's Library, 1992.

Zimmer, Heinrich Robert. *Philosophies of India*. New York: Pantheon Books, 1951.